# Media Choices: Convictions or Compromise?

Phillip Telfer

Media Choices: Convictions or Compromise?
Copyright © 2015 by Phillip Telfer

www.MediaTalk101.org
info@mediatalk101.org

Media Talk 101
P.O. Box 201
Mount Carroll, Illinois 61053
(815) 275-1700

Special thanks to Elisabeth Telfer and Jim & Anne Olson

Cover design by Matthew Sample II

ISBN: 978-1511636322

"Every song is a sermon,
Every movie a message,
Every TV a teacher,
Every word a weapon,
And a picture is worth
a thousand words"

– Phillip Telfer

# Table of Contents

# Endorsements

"Phillip wrote a book?"
– Phillip's Mom

"Will Papa come out of his office now?"
– Hannah Telfer

"He is so handsome."
– Mary Telfer

"You were supposed to say nice things about my book."
– Phillip Telfer

"Does this mean I'm done proofreading?"
– Elisabeth Telfer

"Hey Dad, will you have time to fly planes now?"
– CJ Telfer

"You've got to be kidding!"
– Phillip's High School English Teacher

"I think my dad's book is very nice. I don't get to read it until I'm twelve but I'm sure I'll like it."
– Grace Telfer

# Preface

This book began in 2005 as a series of notes for a seminar that I was preparing to share in churches and other venues across the U.S.A. My plan was to edit the notes and publish them as a small booklet. I kept writing and the booklet kept growing until it had emerged as an actual book. That was ten years ago, and much has changed during this last decade. I realized that I needed to revise the book that was titled, "What Wouldn't Jesus Do? Media Choices in the Light of Following Christ." I spent more than a year re-editing the material and adding fourteen new chapters.

The original book was the catalyst for my introductory seminar which became known as "Media Choices: Convictions or Compromise?" Over the years, I continued to add new material to the presentation and tweak what was remaining. The new chapters that I have added to this book have come from the seminar. It seems as if the process has come full circle and I've adjusted the order of chapters to match as closely as possible.

My original target audience was teens, but I found that the book as well as the presentation struck a chord with all ages. I kept that in mind as I was working on this major revision.

It is very challenging to write a book knowing that the audience will be a mix between youth and adults. I have endeavored to write as broadly as possible, but it was inevitable to make distinct appeals to youth at times, and to parents at other times. I trust that the reader will be gracious to accommodate this approach since it breaks some standard rules about targeting a specific audience.

– Phillip Telfer
April 7, 2015

# Chapter 1: Entertainment: Handle with Care

So many things in this world run on fuel. I live out in the country so gasoline comes in handy around my place, not only for my vehicles but also for my riding mower, push mower, trimmer, and chainsaw. It occasionally makes an effective fire starter for idiots who should know better.

Once I had to dispose of a dead animal carcass, but I didn't want to take the time to bury it in the yard, so I placed the dead animal in a steel burning barrel and doused it with gasoline. If you are not familiar with a burn barrel, it is simply a 55 gallon steel drum with an open top and several holes punched in the side to allow a fire to get oxygen. They are not uncommon in the country and I thought I would make good use of mine. I was about to toss in a match when another thought crossed my mind. This might be a good time to burn that growing pile of chicken feed sacks in the barn.

I blew out the match and marched off to the barn. We were raising over thirty chickens at the time and they ate a lot of feed, which accounted for the mountain of paper feed sacks. I grabbed as many as I could handle and stuffed them into the burn barrel. I was pretty ignorant of what I was doing at this point. I literally crammed as many of those bags into the barrel as I could. I packed them in tight and added a little more fuel for good measure, and then stood back. When I tossed the lit match, I was prepared for a quick flash and a nice fire to accomplish its work.

If you know anything about ballistics, then what happened next won't be as shocking to you as it was to me. The trapped gas underneath the packed bags combusted like gunpowder in a giant cannon setting off an epic explosion! My heart felt like it momentarily stopped from the loud and reverberating sound of the terrifying chicken bag bomb. My sight had been temporarily interrupted, my ears were ringing, my heart was now pounding, and when I started breathing again I gazed up. I had shot all of those chicken feed sacks about fifty feet into the air. It was almost impressive until I realized that I had to run for cover because the sky was now raining large fragments of flaming feed sacks. After dodging the fiery debris, and running around to stamp out small fires, I was left to ponder my careless use of fuel, which had put me in danger. I was really glad no one was around to laugh at my idiocy.

In the same way, have you ever thought about entertainment as a kind of fuel that should be handled carefully? If not, you should. Media plays a large part of what fuels the hearts and minds of our generation. We mistakenly think, "It's just entertainment," or, "It's innocent amusement." On the contrary, it has become one of the biggest stumbling blocks of spiritual growth and family health, and is one of the most neglected subjects to be addressed from a Biblical worldview in homes and churches. The dramatic and sudden change in our society that has come about through this electronic age has unfortunately left many families in a confused stupor, wondering how to approach the subject of media in their homes.

Like gasoline, it must be handled with care and we must start by finding help and direction from the Bible. Too many people have the mistaken idea that the Bible doesn't have anything to say about the unique issues we face today. It doesn't mention TVs, DVDs, PS3 or Nintendo Wii. You won't read about PCs, MP3s, 4G, or Xbox 360. The apostle Paul didn't preach about

Facebook, Farmville, Foursquare, or flat screens. There's nothing about Pinterest, reality shows, Instagram, or downloads. Peter didn't preach about Google searches, YouTube channels, movie ratings, or media multi-tasking. The first Jerusalem council didn't address texting, tweeting, Android or i-Anything. These things are unique to our time but the Bible contains timeless truths that apply to these modern marvels. There is Biblical guidance to help navigate this technical landscape.

The escalating changes of the 21st century haven't taken God by surprise. "His divine power has granted to us everything pertaining to life and godliness, through the true knowledge of Him who called us by His own glory and excellence..."[1]

With such a monster of a topic, where do you begin? For over six thousand years, mankind has been faced with sin, temptations, and distractions that can take a person's focus off of God and His plans. Electronic entertainment has brought about new conduits for temptation and time wasting but the age-old battle for our hearts is nothing new.

---

[1] 2 Peter 1:3

## Scriptures for Chapter 1

—•—

"So then do not be foolish,
but understand what the
will of the Lord is."

### Ephesians 5:17

"But as for me, my feet
came close to stumbling, my
steps had almost slipped."

### Psalm 73:2

"Set your mind on the
things above, not on the
things that are on earth."

### Colossians 3:2

## Chapter 2: Convictions or Compromise?

There he sat, face grimacing, hands trembling, his pulse rising and sweat starting to bead on his forehead. The glow of the television reflected off the form of a young man in a dark room flanked by a few peers cheering him on as his thumbs accelerated to keep up with his racing mind fixed on the euphoric sense of accomplishment. On this occasion the points were not coming from a yellow circle swallowing up little dots while eluding little blue ghosts, but of a city thug who is stealing cars, bludgeoning people to death, picking up prostitutes, working drug deals and shooting police. Could this even remotely be a description of Jesus Christ? Absolutely not! Yet it is a woeful description of many young people today who claim they are following Him. If it's not one of the Grand Theft Auto games, it's killing zombies or aliens, or portraying an assassin. It's not just the M-rated video games, vile gangster rap, toxic top 40 songs, crass country music, or raunchy rock music. It doesn't stop there, consider the banal blockbuster films, trashy TV programs, and the endless hours of inane YouTube videos. There seems to be something wrong with this picture.

I heard a story about a man who was shopping at a Christian bookstore and saw a display of hats that had the letters "W.W.J.D." on them, but he didn't know what it stood for. He was curious so he asked the lady behind the counter what it meant. She explained that it stood for "What Would Jesus Do" and the idea was to inspire people to think about that before making decisions. He thought about it for a moment and replied, "I don't think Jesus would spend $16.95 for that hat."

His response is amusing but it is also worth contemplating. Though we can't know for certain that his assumption was right, it does make me think seriously about other choices Jesus would face in our culture.

Have you ever taken the time to consider what Jesus would or wouldn't do when it comes to today's media choices? Wouldn't you love to get a glimpse of His plate after walking through our generation's all-you-can-eat entertainment buffet? Would His plate be empty?

We have a tendency to want a comprehensive list of do's and don'ts but the real key is found in Biblical principles that can encourage and help strengthen convictions about entertainment in a culture plagued with compromise.

I introduced a couple of words just now that I would like to make sure we understand... principles and convictions. A principle is a "general law or truth from which others are derived." A simple definition of conviction is something you believe so strongly that it will guide your actions even when under pressure. Convictions seem to be rare in this age of convenient beliefs. What are those? They are beliefs that people hold as long as they are convenient.

It makes me think about the story in Acts when the apostle Paul is testifying to a pagan Roman governor while under arrest. "Now as he reasoned about righteousness, self-control, and the judgment to come, Felix was afraid and answered, "Go away for now; when I have a convenient time I will call for you."[2] Notice that Felix was afraid of the principles and convictions that Paul

---

[2] Acts 24:25 NKJV

was declaring. What were those convictions? He spoke about "righteousness"—what is right as opposed to what is wrong. He taught about "self-control"—that we have the ability to make good or bad choices. He emphasized "the judgment to come"— that one day, each and every one of us will stand before Jesus "who was ordained by God to be Judge of the living and the dead."

Those were not necessarily seeker-sensitive subjects for the pagan Roman governor. They are not convenient subjects, and the topic of having convictions about media choices in the 21st century can cause fear, like Paul's talks with Felix. One more important note to make in this story about Paul is that he "reasoned" about these tough subjects, and it is my hope to take that same approach. I hope you do not follow Felix's footsteps by responding with a knee-jerk reaction.

I earlier explained the words "principles" and "convictions", but what about "compromise"? This versatile word can refer to different ideas depending on the context. I went to a dictionary to find an appropriate definition for compromise in this particular context. Here are three that apply: "to undermine or devalue somebody or something by making concessions," "to expose somebody or something to danger or disgrace," or, "something accepted rather than wanted." Do you realize that compromise in your media choices can potentially undermine your spiritual health? Did you know that compromise can expose you or others in your sphere of influence to spiritual or moral danger and disgrace? Are you aware that compromise may be something you are accepting that God may not want in your life? Compromise is giving in to pressure. It is like the weak link in a chain that will break when tested by force.

This generation is under a lot of pressure to go along with the world without thinking twice about the impact that poor media choices and poor use of time are having on our relationship with God and with others. It's time to think more deeply about these issues and not brush them off because they are inconvenient. It's time to set a new trajectory and begin to adopt convictions based on Biblical principles. The next important step on that journey is to make sure we have the right goal in mind.

## Scriptures for Chapter 2

"Therefore if you have
been raised up with
Christ, keep seeking the
things above, where
Christ is, seated at the
right hand of God.

"Set your mind on the
things above, not on the
things that are on earth.

"For you have died and
your life is hidden
with Christ in God.

"When Christ, who is our
life, is revealed, then you
also will be revealed
with Him in glory."

Colossians 3:1-4

## Chapter 3: Fixed on the Right Goal

For the longest time, race day seemed like it would never come. The successive days crawled along like a slow moving freight train while stuck at a crossing and late for an appointment. But now the crossing gates were lifting, and the moment snuck up on Kenny like a person who is awakened by a honking horn from behind with the startling realization of having nodded off to the clackity drone of the innumerable train cars.

Before he could get to the starting line, he had to get into his closet to find that nested luggage set, because this particular race was taking place in Gloucestershire, England, which was more than 4000 miles from Colorado Springs. It takes dedication to travel so far in pursuit of a wheel of cheese.

The insanely steep "Cooper's Hill" is the unusual 200 meter course for a traditional race celebrated for centuries. Daredevil racers hurl themselves down the hill, risking life and limb, in pursuit of an eight pound wheel of Double Gloucester Cheese. Kenny's focus was not only on the prize but also on the notoriety from accomplishing this historic race. He found himself in one piece at the bottom of the hill victorious!

This may not be as illustrious or commendable as the records set by the famous runner, Usain Bolt, or the NASCAR wins by Jimmie Johnson, or the number of Gold medals hanging in Michael Phelps' trophy case from his Olympic swimming races. The diversity of these sporting events share some common denominators: a starting point, a finish line, a desire to win, and focus.

The race analogy for the Christian life is a Biblical one. Keeping the right focus in this race is eternally more important than a wheel of cheese or a gold medal. Think about this Bible passage which says, "...let us run with endurance the race that is set before us, looking unto Jesus, the author and finisher of our faith..."[3] What is the finish line and the goal presented in that verse? The finish line is Jesus, and the goal is to live a life focused on Him without giving up. If you do not have the right focus then the subject of media choices is not going to be viewed with the correct perspective. The original subtitle of this book prior to this revision was "Media Choices in the Light of Following Christ." The part about following Christ is crucial because that is the goal.

The Bible verse just prior to my previous quote says, "...let us lay aside every weight, and the sin which so easily ensnares us, and let us run with endurance the race that is set before us..." I intentionally wanted to emphasize the second part of that verse first, because it establishes the right focus. Once you understand your goal, then it makes sense to lay aside any weight and sin, which can easily ensnare you while running the race. No doubt, much of today's media, entertainment, and technologies have become obstacles and heavy chains that are holding many back from running the race with endurance. Yet merely addressing the problems and issues regarding entertainment won't solve anything that has eternal value if we miss the more important principle found in "looking unto Jesus, the author and finisher of our faith..." Our focus has to begin with a growing relationship with Him. When your goal and focus is Jesus, you don't need a rule that says, "Thou shalt not run with a backpack full of rocks."

---

[3] from Hebrews 12: 2

If you are running the race to win, it will be apparent that any burdensome weight or sin needs to be laid aside.

Much of the toxic media that is being consumed today is symptomatic of a heart issue. Eyes are not fixed on Jesus. It also becomes problematic because much of the media consumption today effectively distracts people from fixing their eyes on Jesus. Life doesn't have to remain that way. Are you willing to take a deliberate break from your entertainment habits and begin to reevaluate your priorities? Are you willing to consider what has been neglected regarding your relationship with God and relationships with others? Are you willing to consider beneficial changes that may be difficult? Are you ready to lay aside the weight and sin that is hindering your race?

## Scriptures for Chapter 3

"Therefore, since we
have so great a cloud
of witnesses surrounding
us, let us also lay aside
every encumbrance
and the sin which so
easily entangles us,

"And let us run with
endurance the race
that is set before us,
fixing our eyes on Jesus,
the author and
perfecter of faith,

"Who for the joy
set before Him endured
the cross, despising the
shame, and has sat down
at the right hand of
the throne of God."

Hebrews 12:1-2

## Chapter 4: The All-You-Can-Eat Media Buffet

When I first began speaking and writing about media discernment, the primary focus was about guarding the heart and mind from compromising content. There's been an exponential shift in the last ten years and very few would disagree that we have a growing problem with media consumption—not just the content but how much media we are absorbed with. Yet, is it possible that there is such a thing as a media saturation threshold? The animated film "WALL-E" anticipates a future where people are continuously fixed on a screen and some are gradually awakening to the need for real relational contact. Prophetic? Maybe not. Insightful? Definitely.

One of the more memorable scenes in the movie is when two men are conversing via video conferencing while floating along in their transport chairs right next to each other. Soon after, the robot named WALL-E accidentally causes a man to fall out of his chair. His overweight body and atrophied muscles leave the man floundering on the ground, helpless. WALL-E not only offers him a helping hand but also shakes his hand as he kindly introduces himself. The "personal" contact startles the man yet he is intrigued as something begins to awaken inside. It's a shame when a robot is more personal than the persons.

Are we that far from a similar social dynamic today? According to a report by the Kaiser Family Foundation, the average teen spends 7.5 hours a day consuming media. It's nearly 11 hours a day if you count media multi-tasking. It has been reported that YouTube has now reached 2 billion video views a day and 24 hours of new video are being uploaded each minute. Nielsen Ratings reported that the average person watches 4.7 hours of television every day. Life expectancy in the U.S. is currently 77.8 years, so if you happen to be average then that would equal 15 years of your life just watching TV. It is estimated that the average mobile teen sends and receives 3,339 text messages per month. Did you know that 43% of 3-4 year-olds have a TV in their bedroom?

Is there a media saturation threshold? Does there come a point in someone's life where a longing for something better, something real, something personal, something eternal begins to break through the never ending digital stimuli?

I truly believe that many youth and adults are finding themselves pixeled out and more aware of a need for personal change. Yet they feel trapped and helpless and are not sure how to find freedom. They are awakening to the need but unsure of the path ahead. Most importantly they are beginning to see a possible correlation between their distracted lives and their distance from Christ and other important relationships.

I believe many today have become like Israel after the exodus: "They soon forgot His works; They did not wait for His counsel, but lusted exceedingly in the wilderness, and tested God in the desert. And He gave them their request, but sent leanness into their soul."[4]

Are you finding that your plate is full at the end of the all-you-can-eat media buffet but your soul is increasingly more empty? Have you found yourself wandering in the digital wilderness and wondering if there's something more to life? Are you concerned about those around you who are struggling to

---

[4] Psalm 106:13-15

break free? Are you empathetic towards those who are numb and unaware that they are exchanging a truly satisfying life for pseudo-living offered conveniently through today's entertainments?

I was speaking to a group of teens several years ago in Knoxville, Tennessee and afterwards a boy about twelve years old approached me and shared openly about the amount of time he knew he was wasting playing video games. I was moved by his transparency as he explained his less-than-ideal family situation and gave some heartfelt insight as to why he was choosing the route he was on. He honestly stated, "I am lonely and I don't know what to do with myself."

I believe he could be a spokesman for a large demographic of youth and adults who have mistakenly attempted to pacify their gnawing internal emptiness through a "diet" that can never satisfy the soul that longs for God. Jesus said, "Blessed are those who hunger and thirst for righteousness for they shall be satisfied."[5] Isaiah 55:2 says, "Why do you spend money for what is not bread, and your wages for what does not satisfy? Listen carefully to Me, and eat what is good, and let your soul delight itself in abundance."

The souls of this generation are lean. They need to be challenged, but they also need to see others who are demonstrating what it means to respond to that challenge by learning to live in freedom from the distractions in this world with eyes trained on Christ. I hope that you and I will be the examples that this world needs; examples of what it means to follow Christ and grow deeper in our relationship with Him. "As

---

[5] Matthew 5:6

for me, I will see Your face in righteousness; I shall be satisfied when I awake in Your likeness."[6]

No real relationship can thrive without regular and personal communication. So if you're wishing you could conveniently find Jesus on Facebook, realize that you won't find His profile until you have your face in His Book. If you're wondering why He doesn't text you, it's probably because you haven't responded to the Text He has already sent. He doesn't need to use Skype, Twitter, Instagram, or anything else that requires an internet connection. The connection He's provided surpasses any global network and reaches beyond the universe into spiritual realms inaccessible to Verizon, AT&T or Sprint. 4G may be ten times faster than 3G but the kind of fast that we need in this society doesn't have to do with downloads. It's not about a strong signal or large bandwidth, but a broken heart and a contrite spirit. You don't need high speed just bent knees.

Are you sensing a need for change? Are you becoming aware of a media saturation threshold in your own life? If you are awakening to a desire for a new life of freedom and personal intimacy with Christ, then start by asking Jesus for the help of His Holy Spirit. He is waiting to extend a helping hand to you as you find yourself helplessly floundering on the floor.

---

[6] Psalm 17:15

## Scriptures for Chapter 4

"And do not be
conformed to this world,
but be transformed by the
renewing of your mind,
so that you may prove
what the will of God is,
that which is good and
acceptable and perfect."

### Romans 12:2

"You shall love the
Lord your God with
all your heart and with
all your soul and with
all your might."

### Deuteronomy 6:5

## Chapter 5: Confessions of a TV Addict

"My name is Phillip, and I am a recovering TV addict..." That probably sounds strange coming from someone who doesn't have a television in his house, so let me explain. There was a time in my parents' childhood that they did not have a television; not that they didn't exist, they just didn't happen to be in everyone's home at the time. They told me that they had a television before they had indoor plumbing, which is a shocking historical fact worth pondering. It has been said that there are more TVs than there are toilets in America which means there's probably more sewage coming into homes than is actually leaving them.

I was part of the first generation to grow up with television as a norm from birth. Some of my earliest childhood memories are vague recollections of sitting in front of the TV watching cartoons. I know that in the past, some have gotten the impression that I have a self-righteous bias against TV because of my outspoken cautions. The truth is—I am really drawn to television, so much that if I am around it I have a hard time pulling myself away. I'm not self-righteous, I'm unrighteous. I have to confess that I am a sinful person and at times find it difficult to turn the channel if something compromising comes on, especially if I've been sucked into the story line. I find myself thinking, "I know I shouldn't be watching this but I want to see how it ends."

How does someone like me end up talking with youth and parents across the country about media anyway? It started when

I began to realize, as a new follower of Christ, that there was only so much time in the day to learn more about Jesus and to practice becoming more like Him. I began to spend more of my leisure time reading the Bible and seeking God in prayer.

Shortly after that, I was invited to an event and listened to a bold preacher share a message of righteousness and holiness. I am not able to quote a single phrase that he spoke that night but I can never forget the impact that it had on me. I began to wonder if there were things in my life that might be holding me back from becoming all that God would want me to be. I sensed God's Spirit beginning to convict my heart about the music I was saturated with and, to be honest, it made me a little nervous. I defensively thought, "My music? There's not a problem with the music I listen to!  It doesn't affect me or get in the way of my pursuit of Christ." I made the best arguments I could but you can never win a debate with God.  The Lord brought to my attention how defensive I was about this and how I was unwilling to give my music selection over to Him. I was reminded of the night that I surrendered my life to God to no longer live for myself but only for Him. He is always right, regardless of whether I believed my music had an effect on me or not. The bigger issue was that I was not open to God sweeping that particular room of my heart.

Music had a chokehold on my life though I did not realize it at the time. I went home and boxed up all of my music and decided to go on a media fast for a couple of weeks. To my surprise, not only did I not miss it, I drew nearer to the heart of God like I had never imagined. Once I was willing to allow the Lord to speak into my life about music, there was a new freedom to invite Him to search through every room of my heart. With the subject of music open to His censor, there was nothing greater in my life, at the time that I would have withheld. I also took a long break from watching TV, playing video games, and going to movies.

What is it that you would not give up if God clearly asked you to? What are you unwilling to surrender to Him? Whatever it is, it is most likely a spiritual bane in your life. It might be the very thing that stops you in the tracks of Christ, unwilling to follow any further. It doesn't necessarily have to be media either. It could be a wrong romantic relationship, it might be unforgiveness and bitterness towards someone, it could simply be an affection for something in the world that you allow to grow stronger than your affection for Christ: a hobby, a sport, a possession, a person, an aspiration, a vendetta, your self-image, money, you name it. If you are unwilling to give it up, then it has mastered you and though you hold onto it or gain what it is you desire, it can never give you eternal life or even temporal life. It cannot save you in the time of trouble, and it will not sit in your defense when you stand before the judgment seat of God. "Therefore we also have as our ambition, whether at home or absent, to be pleasing to Him. For we must all appear before the judgment seat of Christ, so that each one may be recompensed for his deeds in the body, according to what he has done, whether good or bad."[7]

---

[7] 2 Corinthians 5:9-10

## Scriptures for Chapter 5

"Make your ear attentive
to wisdom, incline your heart
to understanding; for if you
cry for discernment, lift your
voice for understanding,

"If you seek her as silver
and search for her as hidden
treasures; then you will discern
the fear of the Lord and discover
the knowledge of God.

"For the Lord gives wisdom;
from His mouth come knowledge
and understanding."

### Proverbs 2:2-6

# Chapter 6: Are You Stuck?

Many children often dream that someday they will be a train engineer or possibly a conductor, but for Rodney and Robert it was a reality. On May 12th, 1998, the two men living out that dream crossed paths with the innocence and vulnerability of a child too young to have dreams for the future, a future that was now in jeopardy. Nineteen month-old Emily had slipped out of her backyard undetected, and wandered onto the train tracks. Rodney, the train engineer, spotted something about 150 yards ahead but initially thought that it was a dog. He laid on the horn hoping to scare it off when Robert, the conductor, suddenly realized it was a little girl. Hitting the emergency brakes, a very sick feeling overcame Rodney, who knew that it was not going to be possible to stop the 6,700 ton train in time.

With little time to think, Robert climbed out of the cab and quickly made his way along a ledge to the front of the engine, perching himself on a small step near the train's snow guard. He thought of jumping off and trying to run ahead to grab her but it was too risky, and she was too low to be able to reach in an attempt to grab her from where he was perched. Finally, sensing something was about to happen, Emily made an attempt to stand up and then crawled off the tracks, but not far enough. She was still on the railroad ties and in the path of the train. With no more time to think, Robert desperately held onto a railing and with an outstretched leg, kicked Emily out of the way to safety. Jumping from the train, he ran to the little girl who was bleeding from some superficial cuts on her forehead and terribly frightened but otherwise alright.

Like a door on a hinge, the ignorance of the little girl, or the tracks of the train, your life can be limited to what you are connected to. This can be good or bad depending on what it is.

Today's culture is largely hinged on media input. It surprised me, after moving out of Chicago, to find the same scenarios and problems among youth in a rural Illinois town over a thousand times smaller. As a youth pastor in this small Midwestern town, it seemed that I encountered everything but gang activity among rural teens. Youth culture is not defined by its location and unique surroundings but by the common denominators shared with the rest of the country. Wherever there is access to television, radio, movie theaters, video game consoles, video rentals, teen magazines and the internet, you find the building blocks of what defines youth culture. This seems to be the case for any setting, rural or urban, rich or poor, East or West Coast. It doesn't matter what gender, ethnicity, height or weight; you can be head of the class or bottom rung on the ladder, smart or slow, gifted at the arts or excel in sports, it doesn't matter. There is a common thread that weaves our nation's youth together despite their differences. It is also what makes it very hard for anyone who wants to follow Christ to get off the wrong tracks.

A person's spiritual well-being and the depth of their relationship with God will be greatly impacted by media habits and choices. Why? It is because media has such an influence and grip on our lives. Ask yourself the following questions: do you recoil at the thought of surrendering any ground? Are you convinced that you can live a good Christian life without changing anything in your current media lineup? Do you think that your media choices can coexist with an intimate relationship with God? Do you believe there is no reason to make any changes and is it offensive to have someone challenge you and suggest otherwise?

I would like to challenge that kind of thinking, but if you are inclined to tune me out, let's imagine that you are right and I am wrong; what you watch, play and listen to have no effect on you or your walk with Christ. The following are some things you should still consider. Having someone challenge your thinking can help strengthen any good ideas you might have or begin to break down bad ideas. This can potentially result in better thinking. In my opinion, that is a win-win situation. If you are searching for truth and have a teachable spirit, it would be a challenge worth embracing.

If your current thinking is right and my opinions are out to lunch then I'm sure you have some strong arguments to defend your views. I would love to hear you, so don't hesitate to get in touch with me. Use the contact page on the Media Talk 101 website.[8]

Don't you think it is strange that people get so defensive about the subject? Even if the argument could be made that media was all good or at least neutral, would you be willing to let go of it if God asked you to? If you are unwilling to surrender even good things to the Lord, they have become bad things because you do not love Him as much as you love whatever it is you are clinging to.

Does it upset you if someone you know refuses to watch a movie because they are concerned about the content? Do you mock someone who mentions that you might be spending too much time playing video games? Do you recoil if someone

---

[8] www.mediatalk101.org

questions the music you listen to? Are you defensive if someone begins discussing your media choices? A missionary named Jim Elliot, who died while trying to share the gospel with a tribe of natives in South America, once said, "He is no fool who gives what he cannot keep to gain what he cannot lose." Jim said that about life, so how much more should we be willing to let go of lesser things? "Then Jesus said to His disciples, 'If anyone wishes to come after Me, he must deny himself, and take up his cross and follow Me. For whoever wishes to save his life will lose it; but whoever loses his life for My sake will find it. For what will it profit a man if he gains the whole world and forfeits his soul? Or what will a man give in exchange for his soul?'"[9]

The person who refuses to allow their pursuit of God to invade their domain of media choices will be the person who will remain comfortable with their media choices and uncomfortable with pursuing Christ at all cost.

---

[9] Matthew 16:24-26

## Scriptures for Chapter 6

"Therefore, prepare your minds for action, keep sober in spirit, fix your hope completely on the grace to be brought to you at the revelation of Jesus Christ. As obedient children, do not be conformed to the former lusts which were yours in your ignorance."
**1 Peter 1:13-14**

"I have come as Light into the world, so that everyone who believes in Me will not remain in darkness." – Jesus
**John 12:46**

"This hope we have as an anchor of the soul, a hope both sure and steadfast and one which enters within the veil."
**Hebrews 6:19**

## Chapter 7: Not Evil but Powerful

I had just finished teaching a group of young people about growing in discernment regarding their media choices when a father who was also in attendance approached me with a look of concern. "Phillip, this is a critical message that you are sharing, but you need to give it to the dads." He went on to explain that he had recently attended a men's retreat and eight guys had brought their Xbox game consoles with them in order to play their favorite video game together during their free time. I was shocked!

That was about seven years ago, and in this quickly changing digital landscape that is like calculating dog years in comparison. When I was a child, the stereotypical dad was the man who got home from work and plopped in his recliner to veg out in front of the TV. Today it's the dad glued to the laptop, the video game, his smartphone, or the TV.

As a dad myself, I can certainly use all the advice I can get to help my family navigate this media jungle. I want to make good use of today's technology to benefit the kingdom of God and to strengthen my family, but there's an important difference between technology and media, and it's easy to get them confused. Let me explain how I am using the word "technology." In the broader scope, the Pilot G2 gel pen that I am using to write this chapter is a new technology. I'm not writing with a quill and inkhorn, nor do I have any interest in raising concerns about the use of modern pens over feathers. When people use the term technology in today's vernacular, it is often in the much narrower scope of consumer electronics. In this book I am using the term more narrowly still as we ponder the use of common electronic devices for communication, education, and entertainment. I'm not talking about electric razors or cordless drills.

When I use the limited scope of the word technology, I'm referring to the devices that we interact with that display some type of digital media. These devices are known as "mediums." A non-electronic analogy would be a painter who uses a canvas, brushes, and acrylic paints as his medium to produce a painting for others to see. A sculptor uses the medium of wood, stone or clay to create a three-dimensional image. An author is indebted to the work of a printer and bookbinder to take his thoughts and replicate them using the medium of ink and paper to produce a book. The finished painting, sculpture, or book is each considered media.

A television is a medium; the TV shows are the media. An FM Radio is a medium but the songs, news, or nonsense being broadcast are considered media. A laptop is a medium but Facebook posts, YouTube videos, Pinterest pins, Instagrams, and Twitter feeds are all considered media. The mediums are the new technologies and the content sent and received are the media.

Just as media can be helpful or harmful, technologies can be blessings or burdens. Throughout this book, and in everyday use, these two subjects are inevitably jumbled together because they correlate to each other.

Technology is not evil, it's powerful. We understand that more power can result in greater benefits when it comes to power tools, but we also have to be aware of any necessary precautions. Smartphones are powerful tools. Think about everything you have access to in the palm of your hand: a phone, a TV, a computer, the internet, a video player, a game device, a word processor, a weather station and so much more. Could you imagine what it would have looked like 25 years ago to have all of this with you at all times? You would be hauling around a cart full of devices and a generator to power them all.

In the words of Neil Postman, "It is a mistake to suppose that any technological innovation has a one-sided effect. Every technology is both a burden and a blessing; not either-or, but this-and-that." He goes on to say, "We are currently surrounded by throngs of... one-eyed prophets who see only what new technologies can do and are incapable of imagining what they will undo. We might call such people Technophiles. They gaze on technology as a love does on his beloved, seeing it as without blemish and entertaining no apprehension for the future."[10]

The technologies are not always the problem. It is often how we use them. If you were in your backyard and you noticed your neighbor on the other side of your fence in his backyard building a shed and using a cordless drill you wouldn't think that you were witnessing anything strange. What if you met that same neighbor later in the week in your local grocery store and he was carrying his cordless drill with him and seemingly distracted by it? What if you said hello to him and tried to start a conversation, but he was too occupied with admiring his cordless drill to give full attention to you for a moment? What if you noticed he was crashing into displays in the grocery store aisles because he was staring at his drill and not paying attention to where he was walking? Would you think there might be a problem? Would you think his behavior was strange? Yet, that is exactly the kind of

---

[10] "Technopoly: The Surrender of Culture to Technology" by Neil Postman

scenario that happens on a regular basis with smartphones today. There's not a problem with the cordless drill; it is how the person is using it.

Our problem is not confined to smartphones. Similar concerns arise when it comes to the subjects of computers, video game consoles, televisions, and other electronic devices. Growing in media discernment does not mean we have to live life without smartphones and other technologies, but it does mean we are in need of self-control and wisdom how to carefully handle these powerful tools. Are these new technologies under your control or are you under their spell? This generation is suffering from its love affair with all things tech, and the results manifest in extremes like texting and driving deaths or less noticeable occurrences like sleep deprivation, inattentiveness to others (especially parents and children), the lost practice of reflection and deep thought, and the neglect of Bible reading and prayer, to name a few. These digital tools allow us to connect and communicate around the world, but have we lost track of the people in our own house and across the table from us?

On the Titanic's maiden voyage in 1912, she had some of the latest and most powerful communication technology, the wireless telegraph. This new technology not only provided critical communication between the ships, it also offered the passengers a new amenity. Imagine being on a cruise today with only one cellphone for all the passengers to send or receive a text message. Not only would you have to wait your turn, but the message would have to be typed out with only one key. To top it off, there is only one connection to use for both passenger messages and critical ship-to-ship communication.

The wireless room had two operators who would each take shifts. The senior officer, Jack Phillips, was known as "Sparks" because he was so fast at sending messages. In the four and a half days until it struck the iceberg, the Titanic's radio operators had sent and received two hundred and fifty passenger telegrams. On the night of the disaster, Jack Phillips, the senior officer, was feverishly trying to catch up on passenger communications when a message came in from the S.S. Mesaba warning of icebergs spotted at specific coordinates.

**9.30 p.m.**
S.S. Mesaba to R.M.S. Titanic and All Eastbound Ships:
"Ice report: In latitude 42 N to 41.25 N, longitude 49 W to 50.3 W. Saw much heavy pack ice and great number of large icebergs, also field ice. Weather good, clear."

**9.35 p.m.**
R.M.S. Titanic to S.S. Mesaba:
"Received, thanks."

Minutes later the Mesaba responded with "Stand by", indicating they were waiting confirmation that the message made it to the bridge. They didn't get a reply from Jack, instead he continued to send passenger messages.

**9.38 p.m.**
S.S. Mesaba to R.M.S. Titanic:
"Stand by."

About an hour and a half later the R.M.S California's radio operator chimed in…

**11.00 p.m. (approx)**

R.M.S. Californian to R.M.S. Titanic:
"Say, old man, we are stopped and surrounded by ice."

Phillips was perturbed at this interruption while trying to catch up on sending and receiving passenger messages through Newfoundland, and fired back with the following message.

**11.10 p.m. (approx)**
R.M.S. Titanic to R.M.S. Californian:
"Keep out! Shut up, shut up! I am busy, I am working Cape Race."

The California was the nearest ship capable of helping the Titanic once it began to sink, but was not able to be reached because the wireless operators had turned their equipment off for the night. Titanic's Second Officer, Charles Lightoller, had been on duty that night and wrote the following in his autobiography…

"The one vital report that came through but which never reached the bridge, was received at 9:40 p.m. from the Mesaba…

"Phillips, the wireless operator on watch who received the message was not to know the extreme urgency of the warning or that we were at the time actually entering the area given by the Mesaba, and are literally packed with icebergs, field ice and growlers. He was very busy working wireless messages to and from Cape Race…

"Later, when standing with others on the upturned boat, Phillips explained when I said that I did not recollect any Mesaba report: "I just put the message under a paper weight at my elbow, just until I squared up what I was doing before sending it to the Bridge." That delay proved fatal and was the main contributory cause to the loss of that magnificent ship and hundreds of lives…"[11]

It is a sober illustration of the potential distractions that come along with the benefits of technology.

---

[11] "Titanic and Other Ships" by Charles Herbert Lightoller

## Scriptures for Chapter 7

"Do you not know that
those who run in a race
all run, but only one
receives the prize?
Run in such a way
that you may win.

"Everyone who competes
in the games exercises
self-control in all things.
They then do it to receive
a perishable wreath, but
we an imperishable."

1 Corinthians 9:24-25

## Chapter 8: Every Song is a Sermon

It's a safe assumption that at some point in your early years you learned the alphabet. It's one of the most important things for young learners to master as they begin their academic education. You sang the songs, colored the pictures and little by little learned that letters were important. Letters came together and became words, and words became sentences, and sentences became paragraphs and chapters and books. It's called literacy, but what is media literacy?

Media literacy is a term that has been coined to describe the ability to recognize and understand that all media has a message, and those messages have an impact in our lives. Unlike reading, we don't need schooling to learn how to watch TV, listen to the radio or play a video game. On the other hand we do need to be trained to recognize what is being taught and the impact of those messages.

Too often we buy into the deception that it's just entertainment. It's not just entertainment; every song is a sermon, every movie a message, every TV a teacher, every word a weapon, and a picture is worth a thousand words.

There's no such thing as neutrality when it comes to media. Let me use the literacy analogy to demonstrate this. If someone decided to write a paragraph using random letters in an attempt to show creative "neutrality" the reader would not be able to discern any meaning from the jumbled letters, yet there is something that can still be discerned and understood about what this "author" is conveying. Their choice to not effectively communicate anything is an indictment that they are not considerate of others, they have a warped philosophy of communication, and have ridiculous notions about how they spend their time and waste others'. Their refusal to communicate thoughtfully is a statement in itself.

Unfortunately, the Christian community appears to be way behind in media literacy. There are more individuals and organizations outside the Christian community who understand the impact these messages are having on our generation, and they are working hard to bring awareness, training and change.

Recently, the National Institute on Media and the Family, released their 12th annual video game report card and the Christian community was embarrassingly indicted for "disappointing complacency" and "sabotage" because of the "disturbing trend" of churches across the country who resort to using video game tournaments with popular M-rated games to recruit youth. In disgust they reported that "allowing 13- and 14-year old teenagers to play games that are rated for players over the age of 17 is irresponsible..."

Why should the Church be more diligent and proactive than the world? Because many of those messages that are infiltrating the hearts and minds of this generation are deliberate attacks against God, against Christianity, against morality, and against purity.

We listen to the pastor on Sunday preach about "loving your enemy," but then spend more time during the week listening to the TV preach the opposite. We read a Bible verse during a short devotion that says, "be content with what you have," while much of the entertainment we consume is intentionally stirring up discontentment. We want our youth groups to emphasize sexual purity while that same audience can often be found munching popcorn in the theater on Friday night being taught about sexual impurity.

It's time to assess our lives and consider if we have been ignorant about media literacy and begin to ask God to open the eyes of our understanding. The Bible gives us an appropriate reminder to take media literacy seriously, "For the weapons of our warfare are not carnal but mighty in God for pulling down strongholds, casting down arguments and every high thing that exalts itself against the knowledge of God, bringing every thought into captivity to the obedience of Christ."[12]

---

[12] 2 Corinthians 10:4-5

## Scriptures for Chapter 8

"For though by this time
you ought to be teachers,
you have  need again for
someone to teach you
the elementary principles
of the oracles of God,

"And you have come to
need milk and not solid food.
For everyone who partakes
only of milk is not accustomed
to the word of righteousness,
for he is an infant.

"But solid food is for the
mature, who because of
practice have their senses
trained to discern
good and evil."

### Hebrews 5:12-14

## Chapter 9: Desensitized and Numb

Imagine for a moment that you woke up one morning and you noticed that your fingers felt numb. At first you may not think much about it, "Maybe I just slept on my arm and cut off the circulation." By lunchtime you are starting to get concerned because now the numbness has crept up your forearm, so you decide to go see a doctor.

The doctor seems concerned and conducts a simple test by pinching your arm, but you don't even flinch. He tries another spot and pinches your arm again, but you don't react. "Did you feel that?" the doctor asks. "No," is your reply. At that moment do you think he's going to say, "Congratulations! We've just discovered that you are an emerging superhero! You don't feel pain!"? Actually, he would be alarmed and begin to order further tests to get to the bottom of the problem.

If you were a comic book superhero, it would not be shocking in the least if you had a resistance to pain, but since you are not a superhero, it should be alarming. You see, your body has a nervous system which does a lot of things and one of those things it does well is to produce pain. Most people don't really care for pain but many times pain protects your body from further harm.

Not only do you have a physical nervous system, you also have a spiritual nervous system which is called your conscience. One of the things your conscience is supposed to do is help you discern good from bad by giving you warning signs when something's not right. It is supposed to produce spiritual pain when your heart and mind are exposed to things that can be harmful. How well is your conscience working when it comes to today's entertainment choices? Can you feel the pinch on the arm?

It is uncanny how many times I've heard these famous words, "It doesn't affect me," when addressing poor entertainment choices. It is often stated with bold confidence as if possessing a particular gift or talent which allows a person to no longer feel pain. That's not a good thing, it's actually a sign of a spiritual disease which is called a desensitized conscience. There is an epidemic of people who claim that negative or compromising elements in their media consumption do not have an effect on them. They are people who believe that movies, television shows, music and video games that glamorize sexual immorality, drug and alcohol use, gratuitous violence, anger, hate, despair, suicide, self-mutilation, greed, discontentment and many other spiritually and morally destructive themes do not have an effect on them. This is not a sign of super human powers but of a hardened heart. The very fact that someone says it doesn't affect them is a dead giveaway that they are infected. No longer feeling the pinch, our generation is desensitized and numb. It is the case of a heart that no longer discerns its own corruption. For many, this has become a self-proclaimed badge of honor rather than an alarming concern. If this describes you, don't panic; there's a cure.

In Hebrews 5:12-14 the Bible tells us, "In fact, though by now you should be teachers, you still need someone to teach you the basic truths of God's word. You have become people who need milk instead of solid food. For everyone who lives on milk is still a baby and is inexperienced in the message of righteousness. But solid food is for mature people, whose minds are trained by practice to distinguish good from evil." These verses are about growing up into Christian maturity. This requires a prior change of heart through a relationship with God, through faith in Jesus Christ, and the transformational work that is accomplished through the Holy Spirit in the lives of those who believe.

Once you have a relationship with God through Jesus Christ, your heart and mind can be trained with practice to discern between good and evil. Maturity means that you are experienced in the message of righteousness, and righteousness simply means understanding and doing what is right as opposed to what is wrong. It's not merely identifying what is wrong but avoiding it. It's not just acknowledging what is good but also doing it.

We don't have to remain desensitized. Our conscience can be trained but it's going to take some dedicated work. That must start with going back to the basic truths of God's Word. He didn't neglect giving us the guidance we would need in order to remain sensitive to distinguish good from evil in today's media. We have simply neglected to recognize our numbness and pursue the cure.

It's past time to spit out the world's pacifiers and get back on the pure milk of God's Word. Better yet, let's grow up and get to the point where we can tackle some solids.

## Scriptures for Chapter 9

"How long will you love
what is worthless and
aim at deception?"

### Psalm 4:2b

"The way of the
wicked is like darkness;
they do not know over
what they stumble."

### Proverbs 4:19

"But the goal of our
instruction is love
from a pure heart
and a good conscience
and a sincere faith."

### 1Timothy 1:5

# Chapter 10: Operating Systems 101

Have you ever experienced compatibility issues with a program you were trying to run on your computer? Maybe you upgraded your operating system only to discover that your favorite application no longer worked. In this digital age there always seems to be a way to work around a program conflict but some problems don't have a quick or easy fix. Compatibility issues with programs and computers will continue to plague us, but these issues are not exclusive to the digital realm.

Have you ever considered that your life has a built-in operating system that has compatibility issues as well? Some would call it your "worldview" but I like to call it Windows MS for "My Self." It is how you manage all the incoming information and experiences in your life as well as what comes out of your life.

Whether you know it or not, this life operating system has been in development since your birth. It is continually going through upgrades, fixes, and tweaks based on your unique upbringing, your environment, education, personality, talents, limitations and a bunch of other influences. It affects what things you try to add to your life and other things you reject or overlook. Your worldview influences what you believe is compatible with your life. It affects the decisions you make in life, the direction you go. More importantly, it affects the way you think about God and eternity.

There was a time in my life when I approached the subject of Jesus as if He were a good program that was compatible with my operating system. It was as if I thought I could keep Him in a separate folder on my desktop apart from all the other areas of my life, especially my choices in entertainment. I said that I loved Jesus but I would expose my heart, mind and soul to music that dishonored God while it saturated my thoughts. I would read the Bible for a few minutes but spend hours during the week watching TV shows and movies that were profane, immoral, or violent. I would say a token prayer before my meals and give my best time and effort towards a high score on my favorite video game.

Somewhere there was a disconnect between what I professed and what I lived. I began to recognize how empty my life had become and how distant I was from God. I was haunted by a gnawing sense that I was missing out on real life. I became desperate to know what it would take to solve the software problems and conflicts in my life. I later discovered that I had a wrong understanding about Jesus, eternity, and compatibility.

My desperation brought me to a place where I could finally learn that true Christianity is not about adding Jesus to my life like another software program that suits my fancy or needs. Jesus said, "If anyone desires to come after Me, let him deny himself, and take up his cross, and follow Me. For whoever desires to save his life will lose it, but whoever loses his life for My sake will find it."[13] Jesus wasn't interested in being added to my life, He wanted to take over my life. He wanted to replace my existing operating system with Himself as the center of my life. I had to learn to deny myself, and ditch my Windows MS.

When following Jesus replaced my life's operating system I began to see things in a whole new light. It was no longer an

---

[13] Matthew 16:24-25

issue about what was compatible with me but what was compatible with Jesus? And that was the start of understanding media choices in the light of following Christ. I began to see more clearly that a large portion of my media diet was not compatible with a life dedicated to following Jesus.

It makes me think about a passage from the apostle Paul which says, "If indeed you have heard Him and have been taught in Him, just as truth is in Jesus, that, in reference to your former manner of life, you lay aside the old self, which is being corrupted in accordance with the lusts of deceit, and that you be renewed in the spirit of your mind, and put on the new self, which in the likeness of God has been created in righteousness and holiness of the truth."[14] Paul had also spoken about this to the Corinthian church, "...therefore if anyone is in Christ, he is a new creature; the old things passed away; behold, new things have come."[15]

Those who assume they are followers of Jesus, but who have not given Him control of their life have essentially placed their idea of Christianity in its own compartment or file folder on their hard drive. That is also why there doesn't seem to be a problem with filling their hearts and minds with entertainments that are diabolical to Christ. They believe that Jesus is compatible to them, but so are violent video games, or raunchy movies, or careless internet surfing habits, or sexually explicit music and culture driven periodicals. That is not true Christianity. You can't just add Jesus to your life. His desire is to transform your life to reflect Him.

---

[14] Ephesians 4:21-24

[15] 2 Corinthians 5:17

## Scriptures for Chapter 10

"And do not be conformed to
this world, but be transformed
by the renewing of your mind,
so that you may prove what the
will of God is, that which is good
and acceptable and perfect."

### Romans 12:2

"Now those who belong to
Christ Jesus have crucified the
flesh with its passions and desires.
If we live by the Spirit, let us
also walk by the Spirit."

### Galatians 5:24-25

"Therefore if you have been
raised up with Christ, keep seeking
the things above, where Christ is,
seated at the right hand of God. Set
your mind on the things above, not
on the things that are on earth.
For you have died and your life
is hidden with Christ in God."

### Colossians 3:1-3

# Chapter 11: An Ambush of Skunks

Of all the ships to lose, why did it have to be the "Nuestra Senora de Atocha"? The country of Spain was left to ponder that question as they suffered such a great loss. The remorse for its dead crew and the eight other ships that sank on the fateful day was eclipsed by the obsession with the cargo of the Atocha, hopelessly sitting on the ocean floor.

The Nuestra Senora de Atocha left Havana, Cuba on September 4th, 1622, with twenty-seven other ships but on the following day was caught in a surprise hurricane off the coast of Florida. The sinking of this particular Spanish galleon was notable because of the 47 tons of treasure that it carried: gold, silver, coins, precious jewels, jewelry and priceless artifacts. It's worth in today's currency would be nearly 60 million dollars.

A salvage operation was attempted right away, and though they found the ship, it was too difficult for divers at that time in history to do anything. The following month another hurricane ripped through the area, and when another salvage attempt was made, the ship could not be found. Over the next twenty years there were several failed attempts to find the ship, but all that remained were the documented maps and treasure lore. The Atocha might have been lost but it was certainly not forgotten.

During the 1960's an experienced diver named Mel Fisher began looking for sunken treasure off the coast of Florida. Having heard about the legendary Nuestra Senora de Atocha, he made it his life's work to find it. This quest would prove to be a costly one. His obsession to find its treasure led to devastating personal loss, including the death of one of his sons when a salvage boat capsized and sank while searching for the elusive wreck. He also endured financial problems, power cut-offs, court battles and other hardships in his endeavor to find the famous Atocha and its supposed mother lode. He sacrificed so much because he believed that in the end he would find the treasure. In 1985, Mel found the Nuestra Senora de Atocha; and what about that supposed cargo of wealth? It was all there... all 60 million dollars' worth.

The Bible says, "How much better it is to get wisdom than gold! And to get understanding is to be chosen above silver!"[16] "For wisdom is better than jewels; and all desirable things cannot compare with her."[17]

The media choices we make can be viewed through the lens of rules and regulations or they can be viewed in light of wisdom and understanding. I personally don't think that rules are the answer for effectively guiding us through the complex issues surrounding today's entertainment. The Bible didn't say it was better to "get rules" but rather "get wisdom" and "get understanding." I hope that will encourage you to find the treasure map in God's Word, which leads to both wisdom and understanding.

Do you know the difference between knowledge and wisdom? Imagine that you are a foreign exchange student visiting the United States. You are enjoying a late afternoon hike in a beautiful park along a well-marked trail, then you spot something you've never seen before. In your path is a small animal that is a little larger than a cat. It has a big fluffy tail and

---

[16] Proverbs 16:16
[17] Proverbs 8:11

its coat is black with a white stripe down its back. You are captivated by this amazing creature and decide to grab your cell phone to snap a picture to send to your family back home.

The problem is that your phone camera doesn't zoom well, so you quietly sneak closer and closer to the mysterious critter. Just as you are about to snap a shot, you happen to snap a dry twig with your foot, which startles your subject. Before you can say "Axe Cologne" the animal spins its backside towards you, lifts its tail and sprays a not-so-fragrant repellant in your direction. What started out as a nice walk has turned into one of those days that really stink!

Now here's what you've now learned about knowledge and wisdom. You didn't have the knowledge that the animal was a skunk, so you didn't have the wisdom to stay out of its path. If you had known ahead of time what a skunk looked like and what it was capable of doing to protect itself, then you would have had the chance to apply wisdom and keep a safe distance or better yet, run in the opposite direction.

Like the ignorance of a foreign exchange student, we often lack knowledge about the impact that poor media choices can have in our lives. Unfortunately, we often expose our hearts and minds to images, ideas, and messages that can really cause life to stink. Worse yet, the intentional efforts by the entertainment industry to influence your life are like taking a walk in a park and then being ambushed by an army of skunks. So how do you gain wisdom? You need to seek it out like Mel Fisher sought for the sunken treasure.

The Bible says, "The fear of the Lord is the beginning of knowledge, but fools despise wisdom and instruction."[18] It also

---

[18] Proverbs 1:7

tells us, "Get wisdom! Get understanding."[19] Did you know that one of the few things we are told in the Bible about Jesus between the age of twelve and when He began His public ministry at around thirty years old is that He grew in wisdom? Luke 2:52 says, "And Jesus increased in wisdom and stature, and in favor with God and men." If it was important to Jesus, it must be important to us.

From the first book of Genesis to the final book of Revelation, God has revealed Himself to mankind. The pinnacle of His revelation to us appeared in the form of a baby who was born to a virgin girl; this was Jesus, the Son of God, who left heaven and all of its wonders to come and dwell with His creation on earth. More importantly, He came to show us the love of God and reveal His plan to save us from the destruction of sin.

The Bible is where we learn about God's character and His attributes, His desires and His concerns, His likes and His dislikes, the things He loves and the things He hates. We are not left to guess about what God would think about the unique things that we face in the 21st century. The principles that can be applied from Scripture are not just instructions about right and wrong, they are about our relationship with God and learning how we can be pleasing to Him. The big question is do you really want to know what God has to say? Do you really want to gain wisdom and understanding about media from Jesus? Maybe you happen to be reading this book but you would not consider yourself a Christian. I encourage you to keep reading. Anyone is welcome to join in this treasure hunt with me, and

---

[19] Proverbs 4:5a

when we find what we are really looking for, it will be worth the time and energy invested.

## Scriptures for Chapter 11

"My people are destroyed
for a lack of knowledge."

### Hosea 4:6a

"Teach me good discernment
and knowledge, for I believe
in Your commandments."

### Psalm 119:66

"And this I pray, that your
love may abound still more
and more in real knowledge
and all discernment."

### Philippians 1:9

## Chapter 12: The Lost World of Black and White

I came across an interesting article called "There Is No Truth." The author pointed out at least 15 things that would have to be true in order for anyone to verbalize "there is no truth." One example follows that it is either a true statement or it is false. If it was true then it is a self-refuting statement which means that it must be false. So at least one thing must be true; that it is a false statement to say "There is no truth." Are you confused? Not nearly as confused as our culture seems to be regarding the subject of truth.

People who don't want to believe in spiritual truth are often those who don't want to be accountable to God. Truth is not decided upon by the majority nor can it be vetoed by any individual. Truth is revealed by God. I use the term spiritual truth to distinguish what our culture is struggling with. They don't struggle with the reality that two plus two equals four.

This generation is the culmination of the Age of Enlightenment (also known as the Age of Reason), followed by Romanticism, Modernism, and Postmodernism. Through all of these philosophical transitions emerged the religion of Naturalism which teaches that only the natural world exists and there are no supernatural or spiritual realities. This gave rise to a religion of pseudo-science to postulate its beliefs in origins and other theories in an attempt to explain away mankind's innate but limited knowledge of God. This naturalistic religion and its so-called realities are promoted by its own prophets as true, and these theories are accepted as truth by their disciples.

When I talk about the religion of pseudo-science naturalists I am not talking about the application of the scientific method[20] that has led to amazing discoveries and has accomplished astounding advancements in medical science, mathematics, physics, engineering, electronics, and more. The problem is that man tries to explain all reality from his own vantage point rather than God's. This affects his understanding of the origin of life and other aspects of biology, sociology, geoscience, psychology, cosmology, and ecology.

This presuppositional agenda to reject the reality of God and other spiritual and supernatural realities have influenced this generation to strive against truths that God has revealed about Himself, about mankind, and about Christ in the Law and the Prophets and the Psalms. Spiritual truth is not popular in today's culture, which means that the topic of right and wrong is equally out of style, because those who are loyal to truth acknowledge that what is right and wrong can only be defined by the Creator, not through scientific discovery or man's limited ideas and philosophies apart from God.

When broaching the subject of wrong and right, black and white, the question will certainly be raised, "What about the gray areas?" I am not denying that there are areas in life and choices we must make that might be considered "gray areas." The problem is not about debatable gray areas, the problem is when God has revealed that something is black but mankind

---

[20] The Oxford English Dictionary defines the scientific method as "a method or procedure that has characterized natural science since the 17th century, consisting in systematic observation, measurement, and experiment, and the formulation, testing, and modification of hypotheses."

contradicts Him by saying it is white or gray. Or when God reveals that something is white and mankind contradicts Him and says it is black. "Woe to those who call evil good, and good evil; Who substitute darkness for light and light for darkness; Who substitute bitter for sweet and sweet for bitter!"[21]

Jesus said, "I am the way and the truth..."[22] and "You will know the truth and the truth will make you free."[23] So if you want to follow Jesus, then you must be committed to seeking truth. It's not an option in the Christian faith. That brings us to a huge transition in this book. It is summed up in one word, "righteousness."

The Bible has a lot to say about the subject, so it would be helpful to know its meaning and more importantly its context for your life. Righteousness simply means "what is right." It is about right actions and right attitudes. The opposite term for righteousness would be sinfulness or simply "sin." If it makes any more sense to you, call it "rightness" and "wrongness." Whatever terms you use, it is impossible to escape either subject if you read the Bible. This is the subject of morality—Biblical morality.

You might have heard that the word sin comes from an ancient archery term for an arrow that had missed its target. My wrongness, your unrightness, everyone has missed the mark of God's intentions for us. "For all have sinned and fall short of the glory of God."[24]

---

[21] Isaiah 5:20

[22] John 14:6a

[23] John 8:32

[24] Romans 3:23

So what does this have to do with media discernment? If you have been convinced that there is a need to grow in wisdom and be discerning when it comes to your media choices, and you realize it's all for the purpose of a growing relationship with Jesus, then it helps to know what God has defined as black and white and what He has revealed to be the meaning of purity and holiness in this world. If you don't believe that God desires you to be set apart from the world as a witness and testimony, then you will likely not be concerned about being holy and righteous.

The Bible tells us that Jesus died for you and rose from the dead in order to make it possible for you to become what you could never be all by yourself—righteous. God's plan was not just to grant you the privilege of heaven, but to give you a purpose through a changed heart that would desire to please and honor Him. He gave you the promise of His Spirit, who dwells in the lives of all those who belong to Him, so that your own spirit would become awakened to what is right in the eyes of God and what is wrong, what is white and what is black, what is light and what is darkness. Those who join the current trend of denying that there is black and white in this world have also denied what God has revealed about His nature and character. You will not find anything in Scripture to support the popular notion that morality is merely defined by personal preference or cultural acceptance. The opposite is true: the Bible gives clear instructions to Christians about what it means to live a righteous and holy life according to God, the Author of life.

## Scriptures for Chapter 12

"Many will follow their
sensuality, and because of
them the way of the truth
will be maligned."

### 2 Peter 2:2

"Teach me Your way,
O Lord; I will walk in
Your truth; unite my heart
to fear Your name."

### Psalm 86:11

"All the paths of the Lord
are lovingkindness and truth
to those who keep His covenant
and His testimonies."

### Psalm 25:10

"So have I become your enemy
by telling you the truth?"

### Galatians 4:16

## Chapter 13: The Counterfeit Life

In 1990, the year I graduated from high school, a much more newsworthy event took place. It was the discovery of the "supernote," a high quality counterfeit $100 bill that had the same raised ink, was created from a special printing press like that used by the U.S. Treasury, and was also printed on similar cotton-fiber paper. This was a forgery that required skilled engineers and equipment that is usually owned by governments, hardly your everyday "funny money" produced by lesser counterfeiters.

Since 1990 there are believed to be billions of dollars' worth of supernotes circulating around the globe being used in other domestic and international criminal activity. Several years ago, federal agents working in an undercover sting arrested over fifty people involved in an international smuggling and counterfeiting operation, and seized millions of dollars' worth of supernotes. To stay on top of things, our government is now changing our currency every seven to ten years, adding more and more security features in an attempt to foil the forgers.

There's more than money being replicated today. The world market is littered with fakes of all kinds. It is not just Rolex watches; there are counterfeit perfumes, computer chips, prescription drugs, artwork, designer clothes, computer software and popular shoes. However, some of the most deceptive counterfeits of our time are not necessarily products or currency. There is such a thing as a counterfeit life.

I'm going to ask you a question and it's not a trick question, so answer it honestly—do you want to live life to the fullest? I hope your answer was "Yes." The desire inside of you to live life to its fullest comes from God. How can I write that with confidence? Jesus said, "The thief comes only in order to steal, kill, and destroy. I have come in order that you might have life—life in all its fullness."[25] Jesus wants you to live a full life and He has come to make that possible!

The problem is that He also mentioned a thief that wants to rob you of this life. Life can be lived or life can be squandered and where you get your definitions of what it means to live life to the fullest matters. Today's entertainment often portrays deceptive messages about what it means to live life to the fullest. The world's definitions of what it means for a teen, or a mom or dad, or a single adult, or a child often contradict the teaching of Jesus when carefully scrutinized. Even when entertainment contains a facet of truth that aligns with Christ, it is almost always presented in a story created by people who have written God out of the script because they do not believe He exists therefore He is not acknowledged. For example, a popular children's cartoon might exemplify selfless love for others, but they portray this by exalting the virtues of mere mortals apart from God. If there is any spiritual or supernatural help along the journey, it is usually the result of magic or mystical creatures with god-like powers.

These kind of portrayals are glittery like fool's gold and captivate our attention, but do not result in transforming the lives of the viewers and imparting righteousness. If that was the case, then the popularity of Disney films and other "good" children's

---

[25] John 10:10 GNB

movies which are memorized, imitated in play, printed on clothes, and sung at the top of the lungs, would produce a generation of nice people who are good and virtuous. That is simply not reality.

Imagine that it's your eighteenth birthday and your long-forgotten uncle shows up to your party unexpectedly and gifts you with a briefcase full of crisp, one hundred dollar bills. Wow! You never imagined being so wealthy. You are too excited to be skeptical and you have just enough wisdom to know that it wouldn't be safe keeping that much cash in your room, so you go to the bank to deposit your millions. Who is surprised more, you or the bankers when their scrutiny reveals that the cash is not real? You have a load of supernotes! You are not rich after all, and besides that, you are now under scrutiny for possession of counterfeit money.

If you are deceived by the false definitions of life to the fullest, you may discover too late that the life you've been living is not the real deal but a counterfeit. How can you identify the fake from the real? The way the experts learn is by studying real money, not the counterfeit. If you are thoroughly trained to identify what is real, then you will be able to identify what is fake. That is why you must study the life of Christ and whatever else God has revealed in His Word for you regarding real life now and the real life to come. The list of lies being propagated through media is much too large to be reasonably addressed in a single book. The following chapters will focus on a few of the common lies being disseminated through entertainment about life to the fullest.

## Scriptures for Chapter 13

"You shall not follow the
masses in doing evil."

### Exodus 23:3

"But the path of the righteous
is like the light of dawn, that
shines brighter and brighter
until the full day."

### Proverbs 4:18

"I pray that the eyes of
your heart may be enlightened,
so that you will know what is
the hope of His calling, what
are the riches of the glory of
His inheritance in the saints."

### Ephesians 1:18

## Chapter 14: Newsflash: God Invents Sex

Wouldn't it be great to be the type of thinker who could invent something revolutionary to the world? Or how about being the next gifted artist to paint a renowned masterpiece? Today, if you invent something, or produce something original, you have exclusive rights by virtue of what is called a patent or copyright. Sure, you could give up your rights by selling them, but until you do, you maintain the rights to whatever you have invented. If it happens to be something complex, you also hold the secret and the knowledge of how or why it works and how to use it correctly.

Have you ever come across something that baffled you because you didn't know what it was or you couldn't figure out how it worked? Consulting a manual would be helpful or possibly asking the inventor. Today there are so many confusing and harmful ideas about sex being taught through movies, television, music and the internet while the Inventor of sex remains largely ignored. If it hadn't occurred to you before, it was God who invented sex. He is the One who holds the patent, the copyright, and special instructions on the subject. God was not shocked or embarrassed at the first couple's love life. Maybe you're the one who is shocked that God approves of sex when it is within the boundaries He has set. The Bible provides all the help we need to understand who and what God invented sex for.

Who did God invent sex for? If you consult Him you will find out that it is clearly meant to be exclusive to a man and a woman who are married to each other. Anything else is a violation of His instructions, and becomes a misuse of one of God's gifts to us. Why? Let's come back to that question after we first deal with a bigger issue regardless of the "why?" If God tells us to do or not do something and does not give us any reason why, we are still responsible to obey. If God says sex is to be saved for marriage, then that should be all the information we need. The Sovereign Ruler over all the universe meant what He said, end of story. Yet that is unfortunately not motivation enough for many who refuse to obey or who find themselves in compromising situations that lead to disobedience, moral failure and the spiritual, emotional and physical consequences of premarital sex, extramarital sex, or sexual perversion. The counterfeit life presented in entertainment spews the lie that sexual immorality is normal and OK.

God wants us to remain sexually pure, but what does that really mean? Have you ever taken a good look at pond water? It's not pure. It's dirty and full of organisms that you really wouldn't want to drink. That is much different from fresh spring water. I grew up in a small town in the state of Oregon where the water supply for our community came from Opal Springs which is regarded by experts as the purest water in the world. My brother works with water as a profession and he informed me that there was a conference where other water experts came from around the world to taste this water and learn more about its remarkable purity. This water, which comes from a deep undiscovered aquifer under a huge mountain has zero particulates, absolutely no contamination. One of the companies that bottle the water stated the following on their website: "Because of its purity, its age and source remain unknown. No trace of man-made substances has ever been detected in its pristine waters. It is perhaps the oldest and purest water on earth." To this day I can go to my home town and drink the purest and best tasting water right out of the faucet. We bathed in this water and even washed our cars in this water.

Like water that has not been polluted, God's desire for us is to remain sexually pure before marriage and after getting married. Purity before marriage means that you do not make your body impure (the Bible also uses the word "defiled") through any sexual behavior. After you are married, you remain pure by staying faithful and keeping all sexual activity exclusive to your spouse.

A friend of mine told me a story about a Sunday school class that he taught for high school students. One week they were having a lesson on the subject of sexual purity and he challenged the guys with the following hypothetical question. Pretend you are ready to get married and there are two women who want to be your bride. You have to choose one. They are nearly identical in every way; they are gorgeous, smart, kind, fun and desperately in love with you. The only difference between them is that one of them has previously slept around with other guys and one of them is a virgin. Which one would you choose to marry? The response was unanimous, the guys would prefer to marry the virgin. My friend then addressed the girls in his class, "Did you hear that? Don't forget it because it is usually the guys who will pressure a girl to have sex with them, yet hypocritically declare that they would prefer to marry a virgin."

It has become a very popular practice for young people to make purity vows and wear purity rings to be kept until marriage. Many churches and youth events even hold ceremonies for it. I think it's a great practice for young people to declare their virginity and commitment to wait until marriage, but purity is much more than that. Purity must begin with the heart and must go further than saying you won't have sex. You are not just a body, you also have a spirit and soul. Your life can become impure mentally, emotionally, and spiritually as well.

A ring and a vow will not protect your eyes from sexual images if you do not understand purity beyond physical sex. The ring will not protect your mind from provocative messages in popular music or give you power over sexual temptation or invoke principles and convictions that do not exist or go far enough. Many youth who wear the purity rings and have taken chastity vows continue to flood their hearts and minds with sexually charged movies, television shows, music, video games, web sites and magazines that taint the heart and soul. These habits embrace a force that works directly against their declared vows of purity. The result is an outward conviction based on a ring and vow that has no internal structure to keep it strong. It's like building a house with only the surface materials but neglecting to build on a solid foundation and with a sturdy framed internal structure. It might look good on the outside but when the first strong wind comes along, it is likely to crumble. For the young person who allows their mind to be filled with sexual imagery and ideas, their outward convictions are likely to crumble at the first real sexual temptation or pressure.

I read an article a couple years ago with a ridiculous title, "Abstinence Doesn't Work, Teens Still Getting Pregnant." I hold some pretty strong convictions that there has only been one miraculous virgin birth in history. How are teens getting pregnant while remaining abstinent? It is obviously a haphazard title for a misdirected report. The article was one of many that has emerged following studies on abstinence programs that encourage teens to make pledges to abstain from sex until marriage. Statistically, these programs don't seem to make a difference. The study found that 82 percent of those who made a pledge did not keep their promise. This report didn't shock me but there is another one that did. In the book Meaningless Words and Broken Covenants author Tim Coody writes, "A recent article in Christianity today reported some alarming statistics about the True Love Waits campaign. In his article entitled 'The Scandal of the Evangelical Conscience,' Ronald J. Sider sites research that followed 12,000 young people who took the True Love Waits pledge over a seven-year period. Eighty-eight percent of the young people who pledged to wait admitted they had engaged in sexual intercourse prior to marriage. Sadly, only 12 percent of this group kept their promise."

The True Love Waits campaign was popular when I was a teen which was over twenty years ago, but there are new school events on the subject of abstinence before marriage now. When I heard about a major one coming to our city, I made it a priority to attend. I was hopeful it would present a solid Biblical message to young adults, but I was skeptical about whether or not they would address media and entertainment with an emphasis on mental and emotional purity.

My enthusiasm grew when I noticed they were utilizing live, text-based polling and the question for the teens was in regard to who had the greatest influence in their life when it came to the subject of sex. The results were coming up live on the big screen and the four multiple choice options were parents, pastors, peers, or entertainment. The pastors were in last place, the parents in third place but over fifty percent of the participants voted for entertainment as the number one influence. To my dismay, this organization did not seriously address the subject of entertainment even once during the two hour event.

This is such a critical topic since the majority of those living in America, including those who attend church, spend more time in front of electronic screens than they do pursuing God through prayer, Bible reading and other disciplines helpful to discovering God's design for their lives. Consequently the majority are also absorbing and living out the false ideas about sex presented in the media rather than the true and clearly defined parameters and benefits revealed by God. The false ideas have very few parameters, if any, and embrace the general philosophy that if it feels good do it.

Through media, our generation is bombarded with images, portrayals and themes that assume and promote the false notions that everyone is having sex before they are married, sex is equivalent to love or vice versa, sex is a natural occurrence of teen or preteen relationships, and there are no negative consequences to even casual sex or sexual practices other than intercourse. On the darker side of the spectrum you find music groups, video games, and other forms of entertainment which portray women as mere objects of sex, many times promoting sexualized violence and   rape, glorifying illicit and ultra-distorted perversions of sex.

Less than one hundred years ago there was a much different perspective in our country reflected in the 1930 Motion Picture Production Code. Every Hollywood film had to meet the criteria of the code in order to get a stamp of approval. Here are some examples of these guidelines on the subject of sex.

"The sanctity of the institution of marriage and the home shall be upheld. Pictures shall not infer that low forms of sex relationship are the accepted or common thing." "Even within the limits of pure love, certain facts have been universally regarded by lawmakers as outside the limits of safe presentation. In the case of impure love, the love which society has always regarded as wrong and which has been banned by divine law, the following are important:

1.  Impure love must not be presented as attractive and beautiful

2.  It must not be the subject of comedy or farce, or treated as material for laughter

3.  It must not be presented in such a way to arouse passion or morbid curiosity on the part of the audience

4.  It must not be made to seem right and permissible

5.  In general, it must not be detailed in method and manner."

Things have certainly changed in Hollywood since then.

A good example of sexual purity in the Bible is the story of Joseph. He was a servant in the house of an Egyptian officer named Potiphar, the captain of Pharaoh's bodyguard.

"So he left everything he owned in Joseph's charge; and with him there he did not concern himself with anything except the food which he ate. Now Joseph was handsome in form and appearance. And it came about after these events that his master's wife looked with desire at Joseph, and she said, 'Lie with me.' But he refused and said to his master's wife, 'Behold, with me here, my master does not concern himself with anything in the house, and he has put all that he owns in my charge. There is no one greater in the house than I, and he has withheld nothing from me except you, because you are his wife. How then could I do this great evil, and sin against God?' and it came about as she spoke to Joseph day after day, that he did not listen to her to lie beside her, or to be with her. Now it happened one day that he went into the house to do his work, and none of the men of the household was there inside. And she caught him by his garment, saying, 'Lie with me!' and he left his garment in her hand and fled, and went outside."[26]

The story goes on that she was upset about being avoided by Joseph so she framed him and claimed that he tried to rape her. Joseph went to prison for being righteous.

The story might have ended much different if Joseph had spent a lot of his time fantasizing about his boss's wife. He didn't contemplate how far he could go without crossing the line. He didn't spend his time stealing glances at her and wondering what it would be like to give in just a little bit. He had real convictions that became evident when he was put under pressure.

Do you remember the simple definition I gave earlier in this book for conviction? It is something you believe so strongly that it will guide your actions even when under pressure. This woman tried to seduce him "day after day" and then resorted to throwing herself at him, but Joseph "did not listen to her to lie beside her or to be with her." Ultimately he fled and though it cost him prison time, God honored him greatly. Today's sexual marketing in media is much like Potiphar's wife. It is persistent day after

---

[26] Genesis 39:6-12

day and throws itself at our society. You cannot passively escape the snare. The key word here is "passively." You need to have active convictions. No one can "handle it" when it comes to sexual temptations so the Bible warns us, "Can a man take fire into his bosom and his clothes not get burned or can a man walk on coals and his feet not get scorched?"[27] The Scripture calls it a war that must be fought even though it may not be welcome. "Beloved, I urge you as aliens and strangers to abstain from fleshly lusts which wage war against the soul."[28] The battle for purity is not just for the body but also for the mind and soul.

---

[27] Proverbs 6:27-28
[28] 1 Peter 2:11

## Scriptures for Chapter 14

"Flee immorality.
Every Other sin that a
man commits is outside the
body, but the immoral man
sins against his own body.

"Or do you not know
that your body is a temple
of the Holy Spirit who is in
you, whom you have from
God, and that you are
not your own?"

## 1 Corinthians 6:18-19

"Marriage is to be
held in honor among all,
and the marriage bed is to
be undefiled; for fornicators
and adulterers God will judge."

## Hebrews 13:4

## Chapter 15: A Tale of Two Fortunes

I was inspired to write a short allegory after reading the following statement by Warren Wiersbe, "Sex outside of marriage is like a man robbing a bank: he gets something, but it is not his and he will one day pay for it. Sex within marriage can be like a person putting money into a bank: there is safety, security, and he will collect dividends."

Jared was anxious to make his way in the world and could hardly wait to leave home for college. He hoped to shake his string of petty failures and overcome his vain struggle to attain notoriety and status during high school. His only claim to adolescent fame was his ability to provide bootleg programs, activation codes, pirated movies and anything else that he found while scouring the internet which might possibly give him societal leverage. In the end it did not buy him friends or clout though he regularly attracted leeches that used him for his digital resources and tech savvy. Jared was not blind to his lack of success and that only fueled his growing desperation to make money, gain friends and pursue the elusive life of happiness. Until that happened, he felt he was missing out on something.

Now in his sophomore year he had a small network of friends, though many of them, like him, were looking for a way to cash in on their computer skills and sometimes lack of ethics in order to get through college. Jared believed he found his ticket to fortune when he was singled out by an upperclassman who had plans for an elaborate internet phishing scheme that would hopefully net big money for both of them if he chose to help. That wasn't all, this guy was full of ideas and seemed to be a mastermind at shady ways a college kid might get rich. He knew how to leverage their knowledge of technology and the ignorance and gullibility of others. All that Jared chose to see was a chance to get rich quick and live the life he always wanted.

Over Christmas break, Jared's family was really impressed with his new car although they still weren't clear on how he was able to buy it. In fact they were surprised about a lot of things which seemed to change for Jared, not all for the better. They noticed he was irritable and fidgety, and was obviously dodging many of the questions that arose about how things were going at school and what his new job was like. They wondered if he was tired from burning the candle at both ends. The previous year he had spent most of his break with them, but not this year; it was all they could do to persuade him to stay one night. He said he wasn't able to get any more time off of work, and to everyone's surprise he announced that it was going so well that he would not be going back to school the next semester.

Early the next year he called his folks to tell them he was being transferred out of state for work, but was so brief and out of sorts that he didn't even mention where he would be going. He sounded anxious more than excited, but they were left only to wonder since that was the last they would hear from Jared for several years. It was ironic that they would finally discover him again on the computer while checking the daily news headlines on the web. Jared had made his mark in the world and was facing prison having been caught in a Federal sting along with two others charged with identity theft, grand larceny, money laundering and a slew of other crimes.

On the other side of the country, Brad was reflecting in awe of the series of events which brought him to a juncture in life that seemed beyond his dreams and in his mind, beyond his capabilities at such a young age.

Throughout high school, his interest in computer science and his love for tinkering continued to grow, especially now as he spent his first year going to community college. He had a knack for troubleshooting computer problems and a good reputation for being available to help others in need. People were often giving him old computers and peripherals that had been upgraded, which he always had in abundance. It seemed providential when he was approached by an acquaintance with an opportunity to help a local assisted living community set up a couple of e-mail stations and give a short workshop for interested residents. It was a real bonus to find out it was a paying gig. Brad wasn't in it for the money, but he was appreciative of the income which would help him pay off some of his accruing college debt. He was so elated with the appreciation extended to him from this elderly community that he genuinely desired to extend his help in whatever way he could.

The word got around town of Brad's abilities and good character. Before long he had a difficult time juggling school and all of the odd computer jobs he was taking on. His concern for helping the elderly grew as he found an increasing number of retirees venturing into the world of computers and the internet with fear and ignorance, resulting in a full time summer job. Knowing that many of them were on limited incomes, he rarely charged what his services were worth and many times would refuse any payment other than a bowl of homemade soup or some freshly baked cookies.

Brad was embarrassed when the local paper did a story on him and the publicity not only strengthened his reputation, but increased his customer base throughout the county. A successful businessman in the area read the article and was so impressed that a young man would work so hard and have a sincere interest in helping others that he was inspired to help Brad out with his own talent and resources.

Brad had never met Frank before but he seemed like a nice guy who wanted to help him out. He had asked Brad to meet him at a storefront in town to pick up a couple boxes of computer parts that he wished to donate. As he was driving there he wondered if there would be anything really useful in those boxes; he tried to be as resourceful as possible, but he already had an apartment full of parts that had his living space under siege. As he pulled into a parking space there seemed to be a small commotion on the sidewalk in front of the store, and as he approached there was not even enough time to process all that was happening. Smiling faces, a few cameras, FLASH, everyone staring at him, FLASH, some applause, FLASH, and then Frank greeting him with a big grin as he introduced himself in front of the store's front door which had a huge ribbon tied to it.

Frank had made several calls to friends and business acquaintances to raise and match his own donated funds in order to purchase a vacant storefront for Brad. Frank's efforts were met with so much enthusiasm that before he knew it, word had spread even further and not only was he able to purchase the building but also office equipment and some furniture. Brad was flush with gratitude and awe at the generosity being demonstrated that he almost passed out. Everyone followed him in as his knees grew weak and he slid into a large office chair next to a desk, completely overwhelmed. Someone offered him some cold water from the new dispenser across from the desk and as he pulled himself together, he was a little perplexed as he stared at the set of keys to the building. Was there some mistake? Why was there a set of car keys on the ring?

## Scriptures for Chapter 15

"Let us behave properly
as in the day, not in carousing
and drunkenness, not in sexual
promiscuity and sensuality, not
in strife and jealousy. But put
on the Lord Jesus Christ, and
make no provision for the
flesh in regard to its lusts."

### Romans 13:13-14

"For this reason a man shall
leave his father and mother
and shall be joined to his wife,
and the two shall become one
flesh. This mystery is great; but
I am speaking with reference
to Christ and the church."

### Ephesians 5:31-32

## Chapter 16: God Invents Sex: Part 2

When I was growing up, I passionately believed that I was going to be an artist of some kind. I loved drawing and painting. I believed it was my niche in life. In fact, it surprised many that I did not end up pursuing a career in art; it even surprised me. God had other plans for me and I had come to the point of gladly embracing His direction at the cost of my own. One thing that did remain was an appreciation for the renowned art of the past, so it was with much delight and anticipation that my wife Mary and I received tickets to a Monet exhibit held at the Art Institute of Chicago. If you are unfamiliar with Claude Monet, he was an impressionist painter who in his later years worked on very large canvases because of his failing eyesight. Some of his paintings are the size of large walls. What is also impressive at an exhibit like this was the security. These paintings are priceless and carefully guarded. Great works of art have been stolen in the past, but it is almost inconceivable that anyone would carry out the absurdity I am about to fictionalize.

Imagine someone stealing one of these large, priceless Monet paintings in order to use it as a drop cloth for a home remodeling project. If you have any appreciation for art, then you would find this foolish conjecture to be infuriating even in its absurdity. It would be ridiculous and idiotic for anyone to do such a thing to something so beautiful and valuable regardless of their apparent lack of appreciation for priceless beautiful paintings. Yet this is how the subject of sexual purity and virginity is often handled by those who produce the core of our society's entertainment.

The world's perspectives on sex that are being disseminated through today's media have been taken so far out of the Designer's context as if to make it something as common as a disposable drop cloth. It has been stripped of all its beauty, honor and value while disregarding the potential and realized consequences.

The question was posed earlier, why did God invent sex exclusively for marriage? The Bible tells us that the sexual union between a man and woman goes beyond a mere physical act, "The two will become one flesh." This is an important aspect of God's invention; it unites the two people as one person in an entirely mysterious but true manner. When a couple has a sexual relationship outside of marriage, their lives are joined in this mysterious bond intended for a married couple. In the majority of cases, the couple eventually breaks up and each partner loses a piece of their heart. They will carry that wound into the next relationship, and if they circumvent marriage again, it only compounds the fracture.

When God created the entire world and everything in it including Adam, He said that everything was good except for one thing. It was not good that Adam was alone. God made Eve as Adam's companion and helper for life, which included the joy, pleasure and fruitfulness of sex, but it was certainly not the exclusive purpose for creating Eve. God didn't say that it was not good that Adam didn't have anyone to have sex with, but that Adam was alone. So many people suffer from loneliness today and they think that having sex will cure that loneliness, but it doesn't. A lifetime commitment between a man and woman who vow to stay together through thick and thin was God's answer to mankind's loneliness.

The Bible also tells us that there is more mystery involved in the relationship between husband and wife which needs to be understood. Marriage is a theatrical stage for the world to watch while the husband and wife play the roles of Christ and mankind. The husband's devotion and love to his wife are to represent the relationship of Christ to his bride, the church. The wife's devotion and submission to her husband represents the relationship of the church to Christ. God doesn't relate to us in a casual way, like the approach of so many regarding sex. God doesn't share intimacy with those who have not given themselves exclusively to Him. Yet God gave Himself for anyone willing to be united with Him. It's very important to God that sex be exclusive to marriage because it represents Him. God is Holy and to misrepresent Him is tragic.

"Marriage is to be held in honor among all, and the marriage bed is to be undefiled; for fornicators and adulterers God will judge."[29]

"'For this reason a man shall leave his father and mother and shall be joined to his wife, and the two shall become one flesh.' This mystery is great; but I am speaking with reference to Christ and the church."[30]

"Now the deeds of the flesh are evident, which are: immorality, impurity, sensuality... of which I forewarn you,

---

[29] Hebrews 13:4
[30] Ephesians 5:31-32

just as I have forewarned you, that those who practice such things will not inherit the kingdom of God."[31]

There are several references in Scripture that clearly state that you cannot live a sexually immoral life according to God's standards and have eternal life. It's that serious to God. That does not mean it is unforgivable and there is no hope if you've failed in this area, but it does mean that God does not play any games.

Sex apart from marriage is a theft of pleasure and leaves the offenders without the satisfaction and protection that God has designed. Each person is left "alone" like Adam was in the Garden of Eden, without exclusiveness, without a promise, without security, without a heritage, without completion, without sacredness and without trust. It short circuit's God's plan and rejects the fulfillment that can only be found in the package deal.

A common question that singles often ask is "How far is too far?" with regard to relationships with the opposite sex before marriage. If you are asking that question you are on the wrong track altogether. It's like trying to walk a tight rope over a deep canyon, it doesn't matter if you are a foot from the edge or half way across, the fall would be deadly. It's best to stay on solid ground. Christianity is not about how much you can imitate the world and still be considered a Christian. It is about imitating Christ and being set apart for the purpose of righteousness. I applaud young people today who wait for their first kiss on their wedding day. They are on the right track and I believe that God honors it. They understand wisdom and that if you don't want to get burned then you better not play with hot coals.

---

[31] Galatians 5:19, 21b

Sexual desire is very strong and if you give it an inch, it will take a mile. Even though our sexual appetite is natural, God has without question called each of us to use self-control. It is not to be treated the same as other natural appetites like the one we have for food. We need food to live and God encourages us to eat. It will not kill you to wait until marriage for your sexual desires to be satisfied. Not only will you be glad you waited, you will discover what studies have confirmed—that couples who wait for marriage are more satisfied with their sexual relationship and have stronger, lasting marriages.

## Scriptures for Chapter 16

"But because of immoralities,
each man is to have his own
wife, and each woman is to
have her own husband."

### 1 Corinthians 7:2

"But concerning the Gentiles
who have believed, we wrote,
having decided that they should
abstain from meat sacrificed to idols
and from blood and from what is
strangled and from fornication."

### Acts 21:25

"For this is the will of God,
your sanctification; that is, that
you abstain from sexual immorality;
that each of you know how to possess
his own vessel in sanctification and
honor, not in lustful passion, like the
Gentiles who do not know God."

### 1 Thessalonians 4:3-5

## Chapter 17: Blame the Cow

There's a deep-rooted legend surrounding the Great Chicago fire that was started on October 8th, 1871. It has gone down in history as the result of a cow kicking over a lantern in Mrs. O'Leary's barn behind her house at 137 De Koven Street. The fire burned out of control for two days, leaving behind over three square miles of destruction. Three hundred people were killed, 100,000 were left homeless and the property damage totaled $200 million.

Obviously no one would really want to fess up and claim culpability for such a disaster, so an investigation was done. The fire did appear on all accounts to have started in the O'Leary barn, but Mr. & Mrs. O'Leary claimed to be in bed at the time the fire broke out. Their story is confirmed by the testimony of two other possible suspects, Daniel "Peg Leg" Sullivan and Dennis Regan. Both testified to having spotted the fire burning in the barn and tried to rescue livestock and property before waking the O'Learys to alert them of the fire. Both stories build personal alibis that could not be confirmed by any witnesses but they at least exonerate Mrs. O'Leary. There were five cows in the barn but they did not live to testify. Then there are the multiple stories about failed communications between the firemen and those on watch that night, which delayed help from arriving. It was later presumed that if things would have gone right at the fire department's end, the fire could easily have been brought under control. When all else fails, blame the cow.

There might be disagreements about whom or what started the deadly fire on that fateful night but there is no question about the damaging fire started by pornography.

"For the commandment is a lamp and the teaching is light; and reproofs for discipline are the way of life, to keep you from the evil woman, from the smooth tongue of the adulteress. Do not desire her beauty in your heart, nor let her capture you with her eyelids. For on account of a harlot one is reduced to a loaf of bread, and an adulteress hunts for the precious life. Can a man take fire in his bosom and his clothes not be burned? Or can a man walk on hot coals and his feet not be scorched? ...the one who commits adultery with a woman is lacking sense; he who would destroy himself does it."[32]

Sexual lust is a dangerous fire that corrupts the heart, mind and soul, and in the end destroys life. Jesus warned that if you lust after a woman in your heart you are guilty of adultery. The scripture quoted from Proverbs is about adultery, but it's also about a heart that is captured with lust "...do not desire her beauty in your heart, nor let her capture you with her eyelids..." The Bible doesn't deny that her beauty is desirable, but it warns that it is a lure to a trap, and once you are caught it is difficult to break free. "Can a man take fire in his bosom and his clothes not be burned?"[33] You will not escape the consequences of indulging in pornography, and a simple exposure to it can work like a highly addictive drug that takes control of your life.

---

[32] Proverbs 6:23-28, 32

[33] Proverbs 6:27

One of the huge problems we face today is not only the milder forms of pornography found in everyday advertising and network TV programming that baits the hook, but the harder pornography that is more accessible than ever before through the internet, smartphones, web connected gaming devices, and cable or satellite television. Years ago a child would only be exposed to porn because of an irresponsible or careless adult or else through peers or older siblings who had irresponsible or careless adults in their lives. When I was in school, pornographic magazines were sold at two stores in my small town and they were not kept behind the counters or in plastic bags. Any kid who had the nerve could browse a magazine and if they were really bold, could even purchase one, but most would not. There was a sense of shame still found in society at that time, but not for long.

The following sample of statistics and quotes[34] were compiled by Covenant Eyes, an Internet accountability and filtering company,

- "In 2007, global porn revenues were estimated at $20 billion, with $10 billion in the U.S."

- "In 2008, as many as 40,634 websites distributed pornography."

- "After an analysis of more than one million hits to Google's mobile search sites in 2006, adult queries were demonstrated to be the most popular query category, with more than 1 in 5 searches being for pornography."

---

[34] http://www.covenanteyes.com/pornography-facts-and-statistics/

- "Never before in the history of telecommunications media in the United States has so much indecent (and obscene) material been so easily accessible by so many minors in so many American homes with so few restrictions." – U.S. Department of Justice In 2012

- Tru Research conducted 2,017 online interviews with teens, ages 13-17, and parents of teens:

  71% of teens have done something to hide what they do online from their parents (this includes clearing browser history, minimizing a browser when in view, deleting inappropriate videos, lying about behavior, using a phone instead of a computer, blocking parents with social media privacy settings, using private browsing, disabling parental controls, or having e-mail or social media accounts unknown to parents).

  32% of teens admit to intentionally accessing nude or pornographic content online. Of these, 43% do so on a weekly basis.

  Only 12% of parents knew their teens were accessing pornography.

- In 2001, a study by the Kaiser Family Foundation discovered among all online youth ages 15-17: 70% say they have accidentally stumbled across pornography online.

- "According to a report commissioned by Congress, in 2004 some 70 million individuals visit pornographic

Web sites each week; about 11 million of them are younger than 18.

- In 2008, more than 560 college students responded to an online survey 93% of boys and 62% of girls were exposed to pornography before 18.–14% of boys and 9% of girls were exposed to pornography before 13.

- According to an anonymous survey published in the Journal of Adolescent Health in August 2009: 96% of teens interviewed had Internet access, and 55.4% reported that they had visited a sexually explicit website.

- In 2010, 14-16-year-olds from a north London secondary school were surveyed. They found: Nearly a third looked at sexual images online when they were 10 years old or younger. 81% look at porn online at home. 75% said their parents had never discussed Internet pornography with them. 96% of teens interviewed had Internet access, and 55.4% reported that they had visited a sexually explicit website.

- In 2009, Michael Leahy released results of a survey of 29,000 individuals at North American universities. 51% of male students and 32% of female students first viewed pornography before their teenage years (12 and younger).

Today, pornography is readily accessible in most homes. The ignorance, absence, and negligence of many parents or guardians has allowed more and more children and adolescents to be exposed, and trapped in the dark and damaging world of internet porn. It is not just a problem with children either, adults are being seduced and destroyed in the process as well. A sales slogan once stated, "This is not your father's Oldsmobile," and there is also a distinct difference in the rampant pornography today from years past. It's not just accessible, it's malicious. Many children exposed to internet porn were not looking for it. Some statistics say that 9 in 10 kids between the ages of 8-16 years old have viewed pornography online, mostly by accident while doing homework.[35] Many times porn sites intentionally use names of popular children's characters intended to display their links in search engine enquiries. Some of these sites are even designed to disable the web browser controls to keep someone from backing out while often loading pop up window after pop up window of pornography.

The porn industry is a big business that generates billions of dollars each year, more than all revenues generated by the rock music industry and country music. It also exceeds the combined gross income of ABC, CBS and NBC. Like drug pushers profiting off addictions, the porn industry benefits from everyone who gets trapped in its web, young or old.

Though it is difficult to live your life in such a careful way to avoid getting trapped, it is certainly far easier than getting free once you are caught. It's not impossible to break away and come clean with the help of Christ, but it is not anywhere close to being easy. If you are already caught in the web, find the necessary help and accountability to gain your freedom. If you have not felt the sting of pornography, do all that is in your power to avoid its snare. You cannot fight it and win. The Bible

---

[35] UK News Telegraph, NOP Research Group 1/07/02

doesn't tell us to fight sexual temptation, it tells us to flee from it. "Now flee from youthful lusts and pursue righteousness."[36]

Once again, lust and perversion are nothing new, they have been around from the time sin entered the world. The difference today is the convenience, the malicious marketing, and the rampant proliferation resulting in a net that is almost impossible to avoid being affected by, one way or another. More than ever do we need to keep our eyes fixed on Jesus. It is tragic when those who have hearts full of lust succumb to the mire of pornography, and more tragic still for so many young and innocent minds to be put at risk for stumbling down those dangerous paths.

Up to this point in this chapter I have been addressing the lure that primarily deals with a person's eyes. This has been known to be a bigger trap for guys than it is for girls. On the other side of the coin is an issue that pertains primarily to girls, young women and even older women who have followed the cultural trend to dress in a sexually provocative way. With a generation of guys who are already struggling with their bent to be sexually aroused visually, the gals often add fuel to the fire through the way they dress, or should I say undress, in public. There are two categories when it comes to those who adopt an immodest style of dress; ignorant or intentional. The ignorant category is a little bit easier to address so let's start there.

Many young girls mimic their favorite celebrities who, more often than not, have gained notoriety, not only from their particular talents, but also for their sex appeal. This is usually marketed for all it's worth because it sells. The clothes

---

[36] 2 Timothy 2:22

merchants join in the game by providing an adequate selection for girls of all ages to play "dress up like your favorite pop star." Once it takes root as chic fashion, many ignorant young girls jump on the bandwagon to keep up with the current style not realizing how they are advertising themselves. This is not as "cute" as many parents think it is. These young girls may not realize why the boys give them attention, but they will like the admiration they receive. In time they will become aware of what turns a guy's head and will be tempted to enter the world with distorted values that conclude that they are merely sexual objects to be flaunted, exploited and treated cheaply.

These young girls need positive role models and caring women to come alongside them to give them guidance. They need to be given boundaries and appropriate explanations. As a pastor I have been aware of young girls and even older teens that were committed to sexual purity, but sent the wrong message to those around them by the way they dressed. They didn't have any intention other than keeping up with the latest fashion. Purity is not just keeping your own heart, mind, and body pure, it is also about protecting others. It's great to drink pure water but it's wrong to poison someone else's.

The other category of immodesty is those who know that the way they dress is sexually provocative. They are not naive. They intentionally use their bodies to get attention. What are they really looking for? It is not necessarily sex. They are often looking to fill a need for intimacy and love, or for admiration and affirmation that they may be lacking from their parents. The superficial approach may attract shallow attention from sex-crazed males, but it can never satisfy the depths of a person's longings. It's like a drug addiction that keeps a person from satisfaction, instead giving them an insatiable craving for something more. Those deep longings are ultimately satisfied through a right relationship with God through Jesus Christ and secondarily from being part of someone's heart for life. Marriage is the only appropriate context for sexual attention. "Likewise, I want women to adorn themselves with proper clothing, modestly and discreetly, not with braided hair and gold or pearls or costly garments, but rather by means of good works, as is proper for women making a claim to godliness."[37]

The following are definitions of modest and modesty from Webster's 1828 dictionary.

**MOD'EST**, a. [L. modestus, from modus, a limit.]

Properly, restrained by a sense of propriety; hence, not forward or bold; not presumptuous or arrogant; not boastful; as a modest youth; a modest man. Not bold or forward; as a modest maid. The word may be thus used without reference to chastity. Not loose; not lewd.

**MOD'ESTY**, n. [L. modestia.]

In females, modesty has the like character as in males; but the word is used also as synonymous with chastity, or purity of manners. In this sense, modesty results from purity of mind, or from the fear of disgrace and ignominy fortified by education and principle. Unaffected modesty is the sweetest charm of female excellence, the richest gem in the diadem of their honor.

---

[37] 1 Timothy 2:9-10

## Scriptures for Chapter 17

"How can a young man keep his way pure?  By keeping it according to Your word."

### Psalm 119:9

"But I say to you that everyone who looks at a woman with lust for her has already committed adultery with her in his heart." – Jesus

### Matthew 5:28

"Therefore do not let sin reign in your mortal body so that you obey its lusts."

### Romans 6:12

"But put on the Lord Jesus Christ, and make no provision for the flesh in regard to its lusts."

### Romans 13:14

## Chapter 18: The Best Internet Filter

In the 1990's the clothing company "No Fear" had their logo and slogans seemingly plastered everywhere—especially t-shirts. For the uninformed it raised some questions about the statement people were really trying to make. The branding of this company was associated with extreme sports, and the ideology behind the statement was about breaking the mold of societal norms by taking risks, being daring, reckless, and fearless of death and the law. Did this cultural manifestation identify a deeper issue to be concerned about? Or was it in agreement with the oft cited Bible verse, "There is no fear in love; but perfect love casts out fear, because fear involves punishment, and the one who fears is not perfected in love"?[38]

Their branding was certainly not promoting love, much less perfect love which is found in Christ, so I don't believe there's a parallel idea, rather a contrary belief that has taken root in our culture. We live in a culture that does not have a fear of the Lord. The person who has not repented of their sins and put their faith in the saving grace of Jesus Christ for salvation, has much to be afraid of, especially death and judgment. But it must be the right kind of fear. It is the Christian who has no fear of death because "love has been perfected among us in this; that we may have boldness in the day of judgment."[39]

---

[38] 1 John 4:18
[39] 1 John 4:17

Now it's time to take your own spiritual pulse. Do you fear the Lord? You might be wondering, "What does this have to do with media discernment?" I am often asked, "What is the best Internet filter to use in the home?" My answer, which is often a shock to the unsuspecting is, "The fear of the Lord." If you do not have a fear of the Lord then computer programs, reporting software, Internet filters, or passwords will not stop you from finding ways around the safe guards. On the other hand, look at how effective the fear of the Lord is...

"Do not be wise in your own eyes; Fear the LORD and turn away from evil."[40]

"By lovingkindness and truth iniquity is atoned for, And by the fear of the LORD one keeps away from evil."[41]

"The fear of the LORD is to hate evil; Pride and arrogance and the evil way, And the perverted mouth, I hate."[42]

Did you know that there are over 100 verses from Genesis to Revelation that tell us we must have the fear of the Lord? In these verses we learn that the fear of the Lord is commanded of us, is demonstrated, is followed by blessing, results in God's protection, secures God's provision, grants access to God's guidance, gives insight into God's heart, produces wisdom, and precedes intimacy with the Creator of the universe. The Bible

---

[40] Proverbs 3:7

[41] Proverbs 16:6

[42] Proverbs 8:13

makes it clear that you can't have a right relationship with God without the fear of the Lord.

This is not just an Old Testament subject, it's throughout the Bible, and though it's tempting to list every single verse for you to read and meditate upon, I will try to limit it to a few key verses.

"The fear of the LORD is the beginning of wisdom, And the knowledge of the Holy One is understanding."[43]

"The fear of the LORD is the beginning of knowledge; Fools despise wisdom and instruction."[44]

"The conclusion, when all has been heard, is: fear God and keep His commandments, because this applies to every person."[45]

Proverbs and Ecclesiastes were written by King Solomon, so according to his God-given wisdom, the fear of the Lord is the beginning and the end! So what does it mean to fear the Lord?

Some people try to soften the subject by saying it only means showing reverence. It does include that meaning but it is not just showing reverence. The word used in the Text is from the root word PHOBOS—that's where we get our word phobia which means fear, alarm, fright, reverence, respect, honor, or sense of awe. It can also mean terror or exceedingly afraid.

---

[43] Proverbs 9:10

[44] Proverbs 1:7

[45] Ecclesiastes 12:13

"God is greatly to be feared in the assembly of the saints, And to be held in reverence by all those around Him."[46]

"Therefore, since we are receiving a kingdom which cannot be shaken, let us have grace, by which we may serve God acceptably with reverence and godly fear."[47]

How do I know this is so important to understand and live out? If anyone could rightly say that they had no fear of God, it would be Jesus. Yet the prophet Isaiah said the following about Jesus, "The Spirit of the LORD will rest on Him, The spirit of wisdom and understanding, The spirit of counsel and strength, The spirit of knowledge and the fear of the LORD. And He will delight in the fear of the LORD..."[48] Maybe you're thinking, "But that's Old Testament!" Then look at Hebrews 5:7, which is also about Jesus, "Who, in the days of His flesh, when He had offered up prayers and supplications, with vehement cries and tears to Him who was able to save Him from death, and was heard because of His godly fear." Jesus demonstrated the fear of the Lord and He was the Son of God. How much more do we need to fear the Lord?

Let's go back to my question earlier, do you fear the Lord? If you're not sure then the answer is probably "no" or at least "not enough." So how do you acquire a healthy fear of the Lord?

It starts with a choice. "Then they will call on me, but I will not answer; They will seek me diligently but they will not find me, Because they hated knowledge And did not choose the fear

---

[46] Psalm 89:7 NKJV

[47] Hebrews 12:28 NKJV

[48] Isaiah 11:2-3a

of the LORD."[49] It can also be taught. "Come, you children, listen to me; I will teach you the fear of the LORD."[50] "Teach me Your way, O LORD; I will walk in Your truth; Unite my heart to fear Your name."[51] It must be sought after and taught. Taught to children and taught to adults who were not taught as children. It must be cultivated in your life. One way that I have learned to better fear the Lord is to read the entire Bible at least once a year, if not more. When you read God's revelation of Himself to us, then you grow in your reverence and awe of Him.

The fear of the Lord is not an ambiguous, undefinable, nuanced theological belief that finds a quiet remote corner of the mind to camp out without rocking the boat and upsetting the soul! Those who fear the Lord know it is not something that drives you away from God, but draws you closer to Him.

"For My hand made all these things, Thus all these things came into being," declares the LORD. "But to this one I will look, To him who is humble and contrite of spirit, and who trembles at My word."[52]

"Behold, the eye of the LORD is on those who fear Him, On those who hope for His lovingkindness."[53]

"O fear the LORD, you His saints; For to those who fear Him there is no want."[54]

---

[49] Proverbs 1:28-29

[50] Psalm 34:11

[51] Psalm 86:11

[52] Isaiah 66:2

[53] Psalm 33:18

"Surely His salvation is near to those who fear Him, That glory may dwell in our land."[55]

I know an evangelist, Bill Hayes, who has devoted much of his ministry over the last fifty years to teaching others about the fear of the Lord. He shares about four levels of attaining a healthy fear of the Lord. I want to paraphrase and condense his basic teaching for you.

Level one is the fear of the Lord in regard to avoidable eternal judgment. It often motivates people to turn to the Lord Jesus for rescue from the judgment we all must face (it did in my life), with or without the Advocate and Redeemer, Who is also the Judge. Imagine standing before the Judge on judgment day and learning that the Judge is also the Savior who was spurned. This is a healthy starting point, but it doesn't end there.

The second level is the fear of the Lord regarding the unavoidable consequences of sin in this life. It is the wisdom which understands that God wants us to walk by the Spirit and not by the flesh, not only for His glory but also for our good.

The fear of the Lord continues with the third level that endeavors not to bring shame to the name of Jesus during our temporary sojourn. This not only means being bold for Jesus, but also to walk in a manner worthy of our calling. We don't want our lives to be a misrepresentation of Christ to the world.

The fourth and final level is the fear of losing intimacy with God. Not quenching His Holy Spirit or grieving Him through foolish actions or careless thoughts from walking in the flesh. This is about the areas in our life only seen by God. No one else

---

[54] Psalm 34:9
[55] Psalm 85:9

knows your heart, your thoughts, or your hidden actions but God alone. The fear of the Lord does not drive you away from God but nearer to Him. It drives you further away from sin, transgressions, and iniquity. It keeps you from foolishness, indifference, and carelessness.

The fear of the Lord is the best Internet filter.

## Scriptures for Chapter 18

"For as high as the heavens
are above the earth, So great
is His lovingkindness toward
those who fear Him."

### Psalm 103:11

"He will fulfill the desire
of those who fear Him;
He will also hear their
cry and will save them."

### Psalm 145:19

"The LORD favors those who
fear Him, Those who wait
for His lovingkindness."

### Psalm 147:11

"He will bless those
who fear the LORD,
The small together
with the great."

### Psalm 115:13

## Chapter 19: Twilight Zone: The Invisible Shooter

Too much didactic teaching can get a little tedious and boring, so I thought I would mix things up a little by writing the following short fictional story. The earlier versions of this book did not have this disclaimer and I received many inquiries about whether it was a true story or not. It is not—just a fanciful idea to provoke some thinking and give the reader a break by including another narrative story.

Gary was on the evening shift as a local police dispatcher in a small rural community when the first emergency call came in. The frantic and desperate cries of the lady on the line would have made even the most calloused of individuals uneasy.

Rod was on patrol at the time when the call came through on his radio, an apparent homicide at 503 Oak Street. He was not accustomed to these kinds of calls and wasted no time getting to the address. He met a hysterical woman in the front yard who nearly collapsed in her exasperation. She was having a difficult time catching her breath while trying to  explain what had happened, but Rod just led her to his vehicle and had her sit down in the passenger's seat and attempted to help her calm down. He had already heard as much of the story from the dispatcher as they were likely to get out of her at this point. He was glad to see Sheriff Miller who just arrived. Before long the block was lit up by a slew of emergency vehicles.

The Sheriff, along with Rod and one other officer, entered the house apprehensively and made their way to the second floor. In the first room on the left they saw the eerie light of a television set casting shadows on a teenage boy lying dead on the floor next to a bean bag chair. He had a gunshot wound, but there was no gun found in the room. The mother had claimed she and her son were the only ones in the house at the time as far as she knew. She had been downstairs in the kitchen and her son had been up in his room when she heard the terrifying noise of a gunshot. When she raced upstairs, she found her son just as they saw him now. She couldn't believe the scene she was taking in, afraid she would find a gun on the floor next to him, immediately the avalanche of shock turned to panic as she raced downstairs, pausing only briefly to grab the phone on the way out the front door. She was now afraid that someone else, armed and dangerous, was hiding in her house.

The officers had been cautious when entering and had quickly surveyed the first floor before going upstairs. Now they felt out of their league as they searched the rest of the second floor, but no one was found. Rod was sent out immediately to patrol the area while Sheriff Miller made calls for further assistance. In the back of everyone's minds was a suspicion surrounding the mother.

The nightmarish evening took a turn for the worse when Gary, at dispatch, received a second emergency call—another shooting on the other side of town. This one also involving a teenage boy fatally shot while in his room; the perpetrator unknown and at large. When Rod got the call, he was beside himself; there was some maniac on the loose in his town. He quickly dialed a number on his cell phone while driving to the new crime scene, "Hi honey... just checking up on you and the kids... yeah, everything's alright, well actually, not really... I'm alright, it's just... I don't have time to talk, are the kids all asleep?... that's good, but keep the scanner off for now anyway... I'll have to tell you later, make sure the doors are locked... don't panic... I'll explain as soon as I can... I really can't talk right now... I've got to go... I love you too... hey, one last thing real quick, make sure all the windows are locked... I've got to go, really... I promise I'll call you with some details as soon as I can... bye."

The State Police had now been called in for assistance, and they were sending out some officers as well as a couple of investigators. When Rod arrived at the house, he was the first one there. This time both parents were out in the yard waiting with a similar look of confusion and fear which he had seen earlier. They were flanked by some concerned neighbors and each parent had a young child in their arms, with faces buried but not enough to hide the heartbreaking sobs. The father was somewhat sheepish about having a gun in his possession just then, but told Rod that he got it after finding his son dead. While his wife called 911, he had gone to the place where he stored it to make certain the gun was there, fearing it was gone. When he found the gun in its place he panicked and had the family duck outside while he rushed from room to room out of sheer desperation and instinct to protect his family from a deadly intruder, but found no one. Rod decided to enter the house alone after hearing that the father had already searched it.

Rod was wishing he would wake up and realize it was just a bad dream, but he knelt in the boy's room and checked for a pulse against hope. It was nearly an identical scene as the one he encountered before: a dead body with a gunshot wound, no weapon, and the familiar glow of a TV screen against a wall in the room. It was very perplexing; the state investigator who arrived thought so as well. Even though they had no leads as of yet, it was unthinkable that the person would strike again with all of the commotion now going on in this small town; but they were wrong.

Gary received a third emergency call... "Please, you've got to help me quick... there's been some kind of accident, my son and his friend have been shot. Please help me, my son is barely alive, I need an ambulance..." Gary was in a panic now because there wouldn't be an ambulance readily available and the nearest hospital was too far away for a gunshot victim to be transported without medical attention. As soon as he got her calmed down enough to verify an address, he kept her on the line while he called for a life flight, then requested an immediate transfer of an EMT crew from one of the other crime locations though fearful of its futility. Next, he contacted the Sheriff requesting an officer to be sent right away. Rod was closest to the address, he got the call.

Sheriff Miller briefed him over the radio with as much information as possible: the two boys had been in a room when the mother heard a couple of loud explosions that she said couldn't be mistaken for the gunshot sounds from the video game they were playing, even if the volume had been up too loud. She was infuriated that they would set off fireworks in the house and stomped into the room to find them both lying there. She said that she does not own a gun, and is afraid that the friend must have brought one. He warned Rod that when she had been asked if there was a gun in the room, her reply was very troubling. She didn't see one, but she was understandably more occupied with her dying son. "Rod... someone very dangerous is on the loose, and I'm afraid they might have more names on their hit list. I don't think it's random and by the looks of it this person is only going to stop by force once we catch up with him.

As soon as the medical team is there, I want you to patrol the area; we should have some more help soon and the state chief is notifying federal authorities. Until then we have to do what we can... and one more thing, stop by Billy's house to see if he's home. I know he's technically on vacation, but I saw him in town yesterday and we could really use his help tonight. He's either not home or he's not answering his calls; I'm sure he's turned off his radio for the week. Just knock on his door real quick when you get the chance, thanks."

Rod pulled up to the house but this time there was no one in the yard waiting. As he approached the house, he could hear a woman wailing inside. He called out to identify himself as he bolted through the front door. Gary was still on the line with her trying to walk her through some basic first aid. He rushed to a room in the back where he found the two boys and the mother. He quickly checked the vitals of the boy not being attended to; no pulse. The other boy was alive but unconscious; the mom had grabbed a t-shirt and was applying pressure to the wound in his chest. There was nothing else he could do to help. They would have to wait for the EMT's. He followed protocol and began CPR on the boy without vitals.

Help arrived quicker than he expected, but before he left he couldn't help but look around the room for a gun; but there wasn't one, just a couple of game controllers and a television screen glowing ominously against the wall. Out of a strange curiosity and a gnawing uneasiness surrounding the uncanny similarities at each crime scene, he took a closer look at the game they had been playing. It was one of the popular games which allowed the player to shoot and kill police along with a slew of other simulated crimes. Tonight he had to put aside his bitter hatred for these kinds of games, and his thoughts towards kids who played them and the parents who allowed them. He was dealing with real-life violence tonight, scenes that would haunt him for life. He was facing scenes of tragic, gruesome death, bitter sorrow and restless fear. He needed to get going, there was a killer at large and he was more determined than ever to find and stop whoever it was. On his way out he had the urge to check the window to see if it was locked but he reminded himself that he wasn't an investigator and he had better not tamper with anything.

As he pulled away, the sound of an approaching medical helicopter almost drowned out the banter of codes being cited. He wished it would have, because there was no further distance for his heart to sink and he felt like it would burst on the spot leaving one more fatality for the night. But he did hear what was going on, though he bordered denial—it was another fatal shooting. At least he wasn't being called out to this one; they should have been able to surround the entire town by now with all the help called in. Though it was nearing midnight, he more than ever hoped Billy was at home. He would've felt a little sheepish disrupting another officer at home on any other night but not tonight, besides, Billy was single and the youngest on staff. The faint glow of light through the front window gave him hope of finding him not only home, but awake. He rang the doorbell and heard someone coming to the door. Billy looked a little surprised but didn't seem put out, "What's up Rod?" The look on Rod's face must have revealed trouble. "Come on in."

"Look Billy, Sheriff Miller sent me over here to ask you to help out tonight. He's been trying to get a hold of you."

"C'mon Rod, you know how it is when you're trying to get a real vacation in, my radio's off, my ringer is off."

"I know, he's not upset. He figured as much, that's why I'm here."

"Sure Rod, no problem. I can help out. I've just been playing a game on the computer all night anyway. I could use a dose of reality—what exactly is going on?"

"You don't want this dose of reality, but you'll have to face it like the rest of us anyway."

Rod filled him in with as much information as he could as Billy changed into uniform and geared up for the evening. Rod seemed so shaken that he thought it would be best if they patrolled together. All night the radio was cluttered with communications, but at least there were no more shootings, and to their chagrin, no suspect or even a hint of the shooter's whereabouts.

Morning brought no answers, just more questions. Their town was swamped with journalists, federal agents, barricaded streets, confused citizens and an exhausted local police force. Billy and Rod took a needed break and sat down at a diner for some breakfast. They talked over what details they knew from the horrific night.

"I can't believe there's not even a suspect in question yet, and the investigators and forensics crews have found almost no signs of the shooter except the victims and the bullets," sighed Rod.

"Yeah, but they're pretty sure it was from the same gun or at least the same caliber of gun," said Billy.

Rod pondered out loud, "It's still so strange—no sign of a struggle in each case yet whoever shot them found a way to slip into the room, get in front of them, then shoot and slip out."

"It has to be someone they knew or else there would have been some kind of scrambling going on in the room."

"I guess you're probably right. It doesn't make sense that whoever wanted to kill them didn't get them from behind while they were in front of the TV."

"You know, that's so bizarre that they were all killed while playing video games."

"Yeah, it is and I overheard one of the state guys saying he didn't think the shooter was someone the kids would have known but possibly some nutcase who had some vendetta against violent video games. His guess was that the guy staked out the kids somehow ahead of time or else just went around town looking through bedroom windows since they happened to all be playing the same video game, you know, the popular one where they play a street criminal."

"That sounds so farfetched! He couldn't have been serious!" exclaimed Billy.

"I'm just telling you what I heard. That's their job to look at it from every angle."

"Look Rod, even I don't like those games, especially since they're designed to let the player kill cops, but I can't imagine even a crackpot going around randomly shooting kids over a beef with a video game. Don't get me wrong, I really hate those games in theory, but they are fun to play, especially with the realistic graphics and unconstrained gameplay. In fact earlier last night, when the Sheriff couldn't get a hold of me, I was totally absorbed in a new game. Someone had sent me a link by e-mail with a short note that said 'check this out.' I wasn't sure who sent it, but I thought it might have been one of the guys at work since it was linked to a law enforcement game online. It was like a virtual street game and you just drove around in a scout car or pulled off to the side of the road to clock speeders then you could pull them over and give them a ticket. Even though I was on vacation, I guess I was missing work. It was fun, I would get calls on the radio and would have to drive around and find the address for whatever disturbance was going on and then deal with the situation. I got called out to bust drug deals, chase car thieves, things that in a normal day we don't really do around here. It wasn't really a shooter game, even though you carried a gun; you could only use it if someone shot at you first, or at least pulled a gun on you. It was somewhat unrealistic though, because I had to defend myself nearly a half dozen times in the few hours that I was playing the game. I only had to fire a single shot at each thug to drop them and in each altercation they either missed me altogether or else I was protected by a vest..."

Rod interrupted, "No offense Billy, but can we change the subject for now, my nerves can't handle any more talk about shootings, video game or not."

"Sorry Rod, I guess I was being insensitive. You had to face the reality of it all last night, I hope the worst of it is over and that they catch up with this guy soon."

"Yeah... I really hope so too."

## Scriptures for Chapter 19

"Do not enter the path
of the wicked and do
not proceed in the
way of evil men.

"Avoid it, do not
pass by it; turn away
from it and pass on.

"For they cannot sleep unless
they do evil; and they are
robbed of sleep unless they
make someone stumble.

"For they eat the bread
of wickedness and drink
the wine of violence.

"But the path of the righteous
is like the light of dawn, that
shines brighter and brighter
until the full day."

## Proverbs 4:14-18

## Chapter 20: For Sale: Violent Nation

I remember the first time I saw a horror movie during my pre-teen years. I went to the theater with a friend that was older than me and we watched the latest slasher flick. I felt privileged to participate in such a teenage cultural affair. My friend was a little apprehensive about taking me along, but I had convinced this person that I was "grown up" enough to handle a horror movie. That was what I really thought at the time, but I was terribly wrong. I had not been jaded enough to handle such a dark, violent, and gory film. My eyes were closed for most of the film but my life had been opened to haunting thoughts and fear. That night I couldn't sleep, and I tried to convince myself that it was just a movie and I shouldn't be such a baby about it.

Unfortunately, my story took a familiar adolescent path towards more violence and gore instead of away from it. Instead of trusting my conscience, I felt the need to harden it to tolerate what it formerly would not. I forced myself to become desensitized. We don't realize how changed we become through the constant exposure to violent imagery.

An acquaintance of mine shared a story with me about a friend of his who had grown up in an Amish home. The Amish do not use electricity and therefore do not have televisions in their homes. There came a time in this young man's life when he chose not to remain Amish. While at someone's house watching television he saw a person shot and killed in an old Western movie. He had not been desensitized to Hollywood violence so his reaction might be a bit shocking to most. He was so troubled by what he saw that he bolted from the house and threw up in the yard.

Our culture is so accustomed to depicted violence that it should be shocking how little shocks us. As computer graphics and special effects continue to advance, so does the entertainment industry's ability to produce more realistic scenes, many of which portray acts of violence. Violence has been around since the first family walked the earth, and violence as entertainment has also existed throughout history, but what does God think about it? The Bible is not lacking in stories that involve violence so what are we to make of it?

I recently witnessed the horrific scene of a head-on collision with fatalities, caused by someone texting while driving. The sound of screeching tires, grinding metal, shattering glass, terrifying screams mixed with the horrible sight of bruised and bloodied passengers, limp inside the twisted carnage, left me breathless and sickened to my stomach. My head was reeling while my pulse was attempting in vain to stabilize.

Talk about the impact of media; not just texting, but also the short video I had just watched. It was a public service announcement produced in Britain by the Gwent Police force with the intent to reach the local youth with a message that warns them of the danger of texting while driving. This short video is so graphic that YouTube has blocked it from viewers under eighteen.

I have to confess that I have regrettably sent and received text messages while behind the wheel at stoplights on a couple of occasions—but never again. I was impacted. Does the impact justify the use of graphic violence in a video clip like the one I watched? That's a debatable subject and one that I hope to address. One of the more frequent questions I receive about media is in regard to violence. It is also one of the most difficult subjects to address. Where should you draw the line? Should there be a zero tolerance? If not, where's the threshold?

So where do we start? We must start with God's word. I recently finished reading the book of Genesis and in chapter four there's the account of Cain killing his brother Abel. Then Lamech kills a man and a boy by the end of the same chapter. By Chapter six we read "Then the LORD saw that the wickedness of man was great in the earth, and that every intent of the thoughts of his heart was only evil continually. And the LORD was sorry that He had made man on the earth, and He was grieved in His heart."[56] In verse eleven we read "The earth also was corrupt before God, and the earth was filled with violence."[57]

It doesn't stop there and it doesn't take long to realize that the Bible is full of violent stories. Sometimes those are stories of wicked people committing violent acts, as in the case of Cain killing Abel. Other times we read stories of violence that is a result of God's judgment on His enemies or even on His own people. Some of those stories have limited detail while others have more graphic content like the one I read recently in the book of Judges that tells the story of a woman who drives a tent peg through the head of a man whom she had lulled to sleep.

So—does that justify gratuitous and graphic violence in media that is geared towards satisfying a violence-thirsty audience? I personally don't believe so, based on my Biblical understanding of violence. Here's one example of what the Bible has to say on this subject, "The LORD tests the righteous and the

---

[56] Genesis 6:5-6
[57] Genesis 6:11

wicked, and the one who loves violence His soul hates."[58] Obviously there is a distinction between the historical narratives of violence in the Bible and someone who loves violence. How does that apply to today's media? How are we to discern what is acceptable from what is inappropriate? That is what often stumps us.

Let's consider some basic principles from the Bible. First, violence in media must be appropriate in certain contexts because God depicted violence in the Bible. Second, God's inclusion of violence must certainly not be intended to foster a love for violence since God informs us that He hates it when people love violence. That should also lead us to consider whether God might also hate violence inserted into stories for the express purpose of feeding a person's love for violence.

Before we go any further, you must be honest and ask whether you have possibly been over-exposed to violence in media and desensitized to the subject. That would be my story and because of that I cannot trust my own tolerance levels to be the litmus test for what's appropriate.

With that in mind it is going to take some wisdom, not necessarily a list of rules. It is going to take some prayer and study in God's Word to help us have a transformed worldview that comes from God's Word and not from our entertainment crazed culture. You may need to take a break from violent media for a while to allow time to be re-sensitized. If you apply that former advice then hopefully the following will help: Intent, Content, and Context. I'll give some examples of questions you need to start asking, and then I'll follow up by applying these questions to the violent video clip I described earlier.

---

[58] Psalm 11:5

Intent: What is the intent and purpose of the violence being portrayed? Is it gratuitous violence that is not necessary? Has it been inserted for the sake of entertaining an audience that is thirsty for violence? Does it seek to glamorize violence or a violent person? Or is the intent to teach a moral lesson or to accurately portray an historical event? Is the intent driven by a Biblical worldview or a secular humanistic view of life? Is there a specific audience intended and if so, why? There are more questions along these lines that you can ask, but these will help you get started.

Content: Even if something is historical or intended to be educational, that does not necessarily mean the content should be graphic. For example, there are many true stories in the Bible of sexual sins that people have committed. That doesn't justify watching a dramatized scene that graphically depicts that sin. What may be appropriate to relay in the right context may not be appropriate to portray graphically. The following quote is from the 1930 Motion Picture Production Code:

> "The latitude given to film material cannot, in consequence, be as wide as the latitude given to book material. In addition: A book describes; a film vividly presents. One presents on a cold page; the other by apparently living people. A book reaches the mind through words merely; a film reaches the eyes and ears through the reproduction of actual events. The reaction of a reader to a book depends largely on the keenness of the reader's imagination; the reaction to a film depends on the vividness of presentation. Hence many things which might be described or suggested in a book could not possibly be presented in a film."

To what extent should violence be graphically portrayed? That depends on the intent, and the context, and sometimes the audience. We need to be careful not to assess this based on an already desensitized heart that needs to be re-sensitized. Many of us have not been careful to guard our hearts from gratuitous violence that has had a numbing effect on us over the years. We cannot depend on our own personal threshold to be a standard for ourselves or others.

Context: The definition of context is "the circumstances or events that form the environment within which something exists or takes place." That's not enough in itself to discern any level of appropriateness until you consider the other factors as well. Good discernment will consider the context in relation to the others.

Let me try to put all this together for you by using the text messaging collision video as an example. The INTENT of the producers was to portray a sobering picture of the potential danger to oneself and others when driving and texting at the same time. The violent crash scene is intended to have a beneficial impact on the audience that could potentially save innocent lives. The intended audience is young drivers. The purpose of the violent scene is not intended for entertainment but for impact.

The CONTEXT is a fictional but realistic scene dramatized to portray a deadly car crash. The scene is believable and based on the growing number of accidents being caused by those who drive and text at the same time.

The CONTENT of the video is graphically detailed to give a simulated view of what happens before, during, and after the crash. It shows the consequences of foolish and avoidable behavior while driving. The consequences demonstrated are not just personal but also affecting other innocent people. The extent of the violence portrayed in the video leaves very little to the imagination. The producers were creative with the violent scene and did not make it excessively gory, but focused on making it extremely tragic and heart wrenchingly dramatic.

Conclusion: My personal opinion is that the video was a good use of violence in media and will hopefully be effective. All media has a message and the message given in this video is an important one. I don't believe the video is appropriate for younger viewers, but if we are talking about teens that drive and own cell phones, I wouldn't hesitate recommending the video.

That being said, I'm not trying to have the final say on this subject or even on this video. I confess that at one time I had been very desensitized to violence but over the last twenty-five years have been in the process of being re-sensitized and more careful with media choices. I'm still in that process.

What about violence in the Bible? I don't think I've ever met a Christian or an unbeliever who said they enjoyed reading the Bible because of its violent content. The violence depicted in scripture conveys a true historical record that was not glamorized for the sake of entertaining an audience. It records the history of many events including wars, crimes, evil acts of men and women, as well as judgments from God upon mankind. In fact, it contains the record of a time that the world was so rampant with violence that God destroyed the entire human race with a global flood, except for one righteous man's family. What you do not find in the Bible is unjust violence receiving praise and adoration, but rather condemnation. A great illustration comes from a story in the Bible about a group of young guys who were bullying one of God's prophets.[59] They were teasing him when God caused two bears to come out of the woods and kill all forty-two of them. The bear's mauling episode is not the emphasis in the story and it does not go into a detailed, gory description of the fatal last hour of the boys' lives. Hollywood could really capitalize on that scene, but the story had only the necessary details to get the intended message across: bullying a prophet of God is wrong and could be deadly. The violence was not inserted to make it more entertaining or more shocking for a violence thirsty audience. It simply told the true story, and the story had a purpose, which in the end sends a message of honor for those who do what is right, and dishonor and consequences to those who do what is wrong.

Many of us have been deceived by the influential nature of media and have adopted views about hate, anger, bitterness, violence, revenge, malice and more which are opposite of what God is trying to teach us in His Word. We have embraced lies and have neglected truth. Jesus taught that the Law of God was all about justice, mercy and faithfulness—three things being trampled over, time and time again, in some of the most popular television shows, video games, movies, and music. Yet we are so numb, and are often unwilling to follow the heart of God and counter the direction of the world.

"The Lord tests the righteous and the wicked and the one who loves violence, His soul hates."[60]

---

[59] 2 Kings 2:23-24
[60] Psalm 11:5

The most prominent example in our culture is the overwhelming popularity of video game violence where justice, mercy and faithfulness are sacrificed on the altar of entertainment. Some of the most popular games on the market are crafted to allow the player to act out criminal and senseless acts of violence against people. The games continue to get more graphic and more edgy as the desensitized gamers get bored with the same old thing. It goes beyond passively watching violence; in the case of video games, the player acts out the violence. Many will make the claim that this kind of activity is alright because they are not actually committing a crime or doing the violence. "It's just a movie," "It's just a video game; I would never do this in real life." Jesus taught that it is not just your actions that God will judge, it is also what is in your heart. Nobody in their right mind wants to be a victim of violence, yet marketing violence has been a money making machine in our nation, but not without cost.

What is the Biblical perspective concerning violence merely as entertainment? God hates it! The Bible teaches us that God sees it all, the good and the bad. He is subjected to mankind's violence all the time, in real life. He hears the cries of the victims whose hearts and lives are scarred by violence as well as their families and loved ones.

If a true story of a person affected by the heinous act of some criminal breaks your heart in the least, remember that you are merely flesh and blood, without perfect sympathy for loss, bloodshed, heartache, pain, grief, or misery. We are able to sympathize with others, albeit imperfectly, because God placed that in our hearts from His own perfect heart of love. God sees it all and His heart breaks over the injustice and violence being wrought by His own special creation. Our hearts should be in tune with His, not the hardened heart of the world or the entertainment industry.

If you want to have a best friend, you may learn that it is important to have shared interests as well as dislikes. It's hard to really be close to someone who doesn't have anything in common with you. Likewise, if you really want to be a friend of God's, you must adopt His likes and dislikes because He will not change to cater to your insensitivities or your calloused heart. Do you really desire the intimate presence of the living God in your life? If so, you must embrace what He wants you to embrace and to reject what He wants you to reject. The nearness of God in your life is not dependent on your perfection but upon trust, a trust that honors who He is and takes Him at His word.

## Scriptures for Chapter 20

"The eyes of the Lord
are in every place,
watching the evil
and the good."

### Proverbs 15:3

"Do not envy a man
of violence and do not
choose any of his ways."

### Proverbs 3:31

"There are six things which
the Lord hates, yes, seven
which are an abomination
to Him; haughty eyes, a lying
tongue, and hands that shed
innocent blood, a heart that
devises wicked plans, feet that
run rapidly to evil, a false
witness who utters lies,
and one who spreads
strife among brothers."

### Proverbs 6:16-19

## Chapter 21: Any Bitter Thing is Sweet

Many people today struggle with despair, hopelessness, depression, suicidal thoughts and a variety of behaviors that stem from these problems including eating disorders and cutting. There is hope found in Christ for those struggling, but to the person who is without a relationship with God, it can be a long and lonely journey. It is a search for a plug to stop the gnawing hole in the center of the soul, but there is no plug to stop it. The hole must be healed and it can only find its healing in Christ. For those who get caught in the swirling eddy of despair, there is a tendency to gravitate towards music and other forms of media that fuel the despair rather than direct them towards the cure.

There's an interesting Proverb in the Bible that says, "A sated man loathes honey, but to a famished man any bitter thing is sweet."[61] In order to better understand this saying, take a moment to think about your favorite restaurant. One of our family favorites is Cracker Barrel. I love the family friendly atmosphere and the home-style cooking. One of the problems is that their food is so good and they serve a lot of it, which makes it hard to know when to stop. They have great sweet tea and they bring out a plate of freshly baked corn muffins and biscuits. There's plenty of butter, honey, and an assortment of jams including my favorite Marion Blackberry jam from Oregon. Many of their main entrées come with three side dishes, so imagine chicken fried chicken, mashed potatoes, gravy, fried

---

[61] Proverbs 27:7

okra, and some fried apples. This is certainly a recipe for stuffing myself silly. Now if you've ever over indulged at your favorite restaurant like I do at Cracker Barrel, what really uncomfortable question does the waitress or waiter inevitably ask? You probably guessed right, "Do you want dessert?" How do you feel at that moment? It doesn't sound good because you are stuffed. I love dessert but not when I'm sated. That's the word used in the proverb, "A sated man loathes honey." If I were to paraphrase this using my restaurant analogy it would go like this, "When Phillip stuffs himself silly at Cracker Barrel, he doesn't want dessert."

You might be wondering what this has to do with despair, depression, suicidal thoughts and media. The second part of that Proverb says, "…but to a famished man, any bitter thing is sweet." There's a spiritual lesson to be learned here. A person who has not found their satisfaction in Jesus Christ will experience a famished soul that will often seek to quench that hunger through things that are "bitter." A starving person will gnaw on shoe leather or eat stale, moldy, and maggot infested bread out of desperation. A soul without Christ is empty, and there is a tendency in some people to gravitate towards bitter entertainment to try to stave off the gnawing hunger; entertainment that is dark, full of horror, depressing, morose, full of anger, full of vengeance and of despair.

On the other hand, if you are "sated" with Christ then even the honey of the world does not appeal. You are full. "Blessed are those who hunger and thirst for righteousness for they shall be satisfied."[62] – Jesus

---

[62] Matthew 5:6

There is a large percentage of our nation living on "bitter" media, which becomes an electronic form of inebriation to deaden the spiritual senses crying out from starvation. So many have become addicted to media as a way to cope. When it comes to despairing messages and themes of hopelessness, chaos, and futility, they often do nothing more than fuel an already bitter heart. I can guess that many of those in the entertainment industry are attempting to relate with a generation that is full of depression and angst, but merely echoing their cry does not bring help or healing, and for some it actually leads to death. Thousands commit suicide every year, while many artists who sing about it, glamorize it, even poke fun at it, are still on tour, alive, and making money off of their irresponsible messages. I'm not saying a person will commit suicide because they listen to depressing music; what I am saying is that media often fuels existing despair.

I am not ignorant of the impact media has on the way we think. My own story could be described as a famished soul trying to fill the emptiness with bitter things. Bitter media, bitter friends, bitter rebellion, and more.

I grew up in a loving Christian home where we attended church at least three times a week along with the monthly Baptist business meetings. We were dedicated. My parents were not just Sunday Christians, they lived out their faith on Monday through Saturday and though they were far from perfect, they were certainly not hypocrites.

Unfortunately, I was the wayward son out of three boys, a real black sheep in the family. I fell in with the wrong crowd at school at an early age, and my own sinful desires continued to rule my life. During that time, the media I indulged in had a huge influence on me, and it wasn't for the better. My parents had reasonable rules in our house about what we could watch, listen to, or play, but I always found a way to break the rules or skirt around them in secrecy. It was not just the music I listened to, but also the movies I watched, the games I played, and the books and magazines I gravitated towards.

By the time I had reached High School I began to struggle with despair, depression and suicidal thoughts. I wish I could tell you exactly why, but I can't. I believe it was a cocktail of things going on: drugs, occult experimentation, bitterness, loneliness, and spiritual forces at work. The Bible says "The thief comes to kill, to steal and to destroy,"[63] and "Your adversary, the devil, prowls around like a roaring lion, seeking someone to devour."[64] One obvious factor in my life was the influence of toxic media which seemed to fuel my obsession to end my life even though I was afraid to die. There was this overwhelming desire to cease existing, yet a deep desire to find life. I fantasized about killing myself. I sometimes carried a razor blade with me during this time of my life. One time when I was alone, I started making slight scratches across my wrist and on my arm. Slight scratches over and over until the skin would just start to bleed and then I stopped, asking myself if I could really go through with it.

Of course I didn't go through with it or even attempt suicide, but the desire to die would continue to haunt me off and on for the next three years. After my freshman year, I no longer tried cutting myself; it was not something I had ever heard of anyone doing at the time as an outlet for internal pain—I just did it. Now more than twenty years later I am hearing about it all the

---

[63] John 10:10a
[64] 1 Peter 5:8b

time and I believe I can relate to some of the driving forces behind the trend. That would all change.

Words could not describe the avalanche of emotion that pummeled me one night during my senior year of high school that sent me into a tailspin of depression and despair, suffocating what little desire that was in me to live. I walked home, it was after midnight, I was dejected and numb and had no intention of seeing another morning. Adults will sometimes wonder why a young person can get so caught up with such trivial things, but at seventeen years old, these are not trivial things. They are often the sum of life itself.

I quietly slipped into my room and began to consider what I should do before ending my life. Should I leave a note? Should I... my heart was broken, my will was decimated, my mind was not right, but my soul began to cry out instinctively to God. I began to pray. "God, I'm in trouble... there's no hope for me... I'm a wreck and I want to die... I don't want to live another day..." You might imagine my surprise when all of a sudden I sensed the presence of God in my room, I was sure that His eyes and ears were turned to me... and then He spoke.

It was not an audible voice that I could hear with my ears but it was spoken to my soul and I could hear it clearly. "Phillip, you need to die, but not in the way you are thinking. You are living for yourself and in order to find the life you are looking for, you must die to yourself and find life in Me." I had probably heard something along those lines preached before, but they did not have the power these words had at this moment. Hope stirred in the depths of my being. A flood of understanding poured into my heart as I realized that real life could only be found in following Jesus Christ. He had said it very clearly to His disciples, "For whoever wishes to save his life will lose it; but whoever loses his life for My sake will find it,"[65] and "If anyone wishes to come after Me, he must deny himself, and take up his cross and follow Me... for what will it profit a man if he gains the whole world and forfeits his soul? Or what will a man give in exchange for his soul?"[66] I had learned a lot about Christ while growing up, but I had not come to a place where I was ready to abandon all to follow Him. I was ready to end my physical life, but I ended up dying in a much different way that resulted in true life.

At seventeen, I turned my eyes to the Lord in a time of desperation and received life-transforming grace and mercy from God the Father through Jesus Christ. Thank God for praying parents.

Shortly after that time, I became convicted about my media choices and I decided to go on a two-week media fast. This was a subsequent revolutionary event in my life that would inspire a whole new trajectory of media consumption. I had been the typical teen who says, "But it doesn't affect me!" My eyes were opened and I realized that I was ignorant and wrong. I began a new journey of being re-sensitized to things that I had become desensitized towards, and my heart and mind were undergoing a steady transformation.

Over the next several years I discovered that many people in the Church were not interested in hearing a testimony about media discernment and making wise choices. In fact, many were caustic about the subject and I realized that it was a sacred cow and hot button. I decided to continue to live differently, but quietly, until I ended up serving as a youth pastor for several years. My growing awareness of the influence of media in our

---

[65] Matthew 16:25

[66] Matthew 16:24, 26

culture opened a new chapter in my life. Not speaking up was no longer an option.

## Scriptures for Chapter 21

Why are you in despair,
O my soul? And why have
you become disturbed
within me? Hope in God, for
I shall yet praise Him, The
help of my countenance
and my God.

### Psalm 42:11

"For without faith
it is impossible to please Him.
For he who comes to God must
believe that He is, and that
He is a rewarder of those
who seek Him."

### Hebrews 11:6

"Only fear the Lord and serve
Him in truth with all your heart;
for consider what great things
He has done for you."

### 1 Samuel 12:24

## Chapter 22: Drivers Ed for the World Wide Web

Johnny is eight years old. He lives in the suburbs of a large city and collects Matchbox cars and builds amazing creations with LEGO bricks. One day he asked his mom for the keys of the car. His mom's perplexed reply was, "Why?" Johnny replied, "Because I want to drive the car." She gasped with dismayed shock, "This is some joke, right?" He firmly stated, "No, I'm not joking. I want to drive the car." Johnny's mom was exasperated by this, "You can't drive the car, that's nonsense!" He didn't relent, "Why not?" She didn't relent, "Because it's nonsense!" He volleyed with another, "But why?" And she deftly explained, "It's not legal, and even if it was, you don't know how to drive! You couldn't even reach the pedals! It's not safe; you would get into an accident and injure or kill yourself, and be a threat to others. What in the world makes you think this would be something I would allow or even consider?!" This burst from mom did not sway Johnny as he made his appeal, "Mom, all of my friends are allowed to drive and I've been riding in a car since I was born, plus I've watched you and Dad drive so I know I could do it." His mom was nearly speechless at this absurdity, but she gathered her thoughts and said, "Whether you could drive or not is beside the point. Driving can be dangerous and you need to wait until you are of legal age before you get your permit to start drivers training, and then you will be able to drive under adult supervision until you meet the requirements and can pass a driving exam. That's the end of it!" Johnny relented and contented himself to play with his toy cars.

This, of course, seems to be a ridiculous scenario. No doubt, kids that grow up on farms have demonstrated that they are capable of driving tractors and other vehicles, yet there are good reasons why all fifty states require a written test, supervised practice, and a driving test; not to mention age limits.

There's a reason that car insurance is high for young people. There's a reason there is such a thing as Driver's Education Courses. For homeschool families like mine it's even more challenging because the Driver's Ed courses are often run through the government schools. In Texas, where we now live, it is possible to teach the course at home if you work with a qualified program. I recently signed my oldest daughter up for such a course and I appreciate the resources that they have provided: lessons, tests, driving instructions and more.

By now you are wondering why I diverted from media to talk about driving. I haven't diverted, I'm going somewhere with this. It has occurred to me that this analogy fits the approach I have taken in my home in regard to the Internet. My eight-year-old does not have a "license to drive" on the World Wide Web. Parents have often asked me for advice about handling Internet in the home with children. They usually ask after they have had an internet disaster with a child getting on pornographic websites, or becoming obsessed with social network websites or online games. I am certainly not a child raising expert but I'm glad to share our approach, which is similar to getting a driver's license. Too many parents have handed the keys of the car, so to speak, over to their eight-year-olds and they wonder why the car has been crashed.

My home is not a media-free zone but it is media limited, especially in regard to the Internet. I do not allow my young children unfettered access to the Web. In fact, the only experience they have is similar to the experience most children have with cars – they watch Dad and Mom drive. My goal is not to keep them from the internet during their sojourn in our home, but to help equip them to learn how to be a "collision-free driver" when using the web. We have age restrictions for using the web alone just like all fifty states have restrictions for young drivers. The first stage is supervised exposure to the web, Mom or Dad are in the driver's seat and the child is simply a passenger along for the ride. Just like driving in a car, it is important for the parent to model good habits because much of what they're learning is caught rather than taught. The second stage is much like a learner's permit where a young person gets permission to drive with supervision. They are in the driver's seat, but there is a responsible adult with them monitoring their activity. The final stage is the privilege and responsibility of driving without supervision, but with a commitment to following rules and guidelines. This may seem over simplistic to some, but simple does not mean easy.

Why would this model be difficult for many if not most families today? The big reason is that society in general has not thought this through very deeply and has been very permissive in regard to children and the internet. A majority of families allow their young children to have unfettered access to the internet or limited but unsupervised access. Many children are allowed to play with smartphones and tablets or video game devices that are connected to the internet. These appetites and habits that are allowed to form at a young age don't decrease as the child gets older, they increase. It is the exception rather than the rule to find a teen without a cellphone. It is growing more common to see them with internet-connected smartphones. The direction that I have led my family is certainly countercultural.

As a representative of Generation X, I had enough trouble during my teen years without the internet, or e-mail, or cellphones, texting, tweeting, social networks, and YouTube. The only concept I had of the internet was from a film in the 80's called "War Games" and during my senior year of high school, my best friend's dad had the Internet at home because he had a particular role in the military, which required it. It did not seem that interesting at the time. I was the part of the culture known now as Digital Immigrants who would migrate into the world of the Internet and home computers, which were followed by the invasion of innumerable devices that would become embedded in culture around the world. Those of us who are Digital Immigrants know that it is not only possible to live without these things (because we did), but are now reflecting on how life was more simple without them. That doesn't make it easy to regulate them carefully in our own life, which also makes it a challenge to be mentors for the Digital Natives like my children who have not known life without the Web or a home computer or a cellphone in the home.

What are the concerns that someone should have when desiring to be a mentor of this next generation? Let's go back to the driving analogy for a moment. If you wanted to help a student become a collision-free driver in this fast paced society that often lacks discretion in driving, patience, or even attention to others, where would you start? Probably by teaching them about the common dangers and rookie mistakes. Parents and church leaders need to help this generation understand the importance of accountability on the Web, how to conduct safe searches, the problem and trap of pornography, privacy, age appropriate restrictions, e-mail etiquette, online bullying, misinformation, phishing schemes, predators, and more. This subject really deserves an entire book rather than a chapter and I hope to pursue that sometime in the future. In the meantime, I hope this chapter will kick start some thinking on the subject and inspire a new trajectory for many families and individuals.

There is so much wisdom that can be found in the Bible, especially in the Proverbs, which can be applied to this media saturated world we live in. One of many examples I've come across is found in Proverbs 4:25-27 which says, "Let your eyes look straight ahead, and your eyelids look right before you. Ponder the path of your feet, and let all your ways be established. Do not turn to the right of the left: Remove your foot from evil." The Internet is not necessarily evil; there is much good that can be found if your ways are "established." One simple way to keep out of trouble on the Internet is to have a good purpose that is established before you even open a browser. I believe that "surfing" the web is foolish. It is not only a huge time-sink, but beyond that there are innumerable stumbling blocks around every corner. When you get on the Internet with no clear purpose, and especially no good purpose, then your way is not established and your feet may find themselves entering "the path of the wicked."[67]

I teach my children that the Web is like the local library, we go there at times but we don't read or checkout just any book. In fact there are many books we will not even look at. The reason is that there are books that are "in the way of evil,"[68] which we are instructed to "avoid it, do not travel on it; turn away from it

---

[67] Proverbs 4:14
[68] Proverbs 4:14

and pass on."[69] When we go to the local library, we already have books in mind that we will check out. Our way is established.

We are told in the book of Hebrews that Christian maturity comes from training our senses to discern between good and evil. Just as much as our children will need to be trained to be collision free drivers, we need to train them to not "turn to the right or the left" when utilizing the powerful resource of the Internet.

---

[69] Proverbs 4:15

## Scriptures for Chapter 22

"Whoever is wise, let him understand these things; whoever is discerning, let him know them. For the ways of the Lord are right, and the righteous will walk in them, but transgressors will stumble in them."

### Hosea 14:9

"Lead me in Your truth and teach me, for You are the God of my salvation; for You I wait all the day."

### Psalm 25:5

"Turn away my eyes from looking at vanity, and revive me in Your ways."

### Psalm 119:37

"Act as free men, and do not use your freedom as a covering for evil, but use it as bondslaves of God."

### 1 Peter 2:16

## Chapter 23: Be Filled with the Spirit

Several years ago I had been invited to lead worship at a church in Naples, Florida for a Sunday morning service. I arrived the day before and the church booked a hotel room for me at a nice place near the beach. The not-so-nice part of this was the loud party happening late that night outside my beach-level room while I was trying to get some sleep. I was almost ready to call the front desk and ask to be moved to a different room, but that would mean packing up and walking past all the partiers in obvious frustration. That's when the Holy Spirit began to convict me that I was more concerned about sleep than souls. I got up, got dressed, grabbed my guitar and joined them.

I was greeted with exuberant enthusiasm over the prospect of live music for their party. They immediately began requesting their favorite songs, but they were in for a surprise when I explained that I was a singer-songwriter and only played original music. Their enthusiasm didn't abate but actually heightened for the time being, and I was welcomed to sing a song. I started with one called "I Raise a White Flag," which was one of my more popular songs at the time, and it tells my story of surrendering to Jesus Christ. When the song was over, they were stunned. Partly because they thought I was much better than they had anticipated, but more so because of the clear Christian message. They were literally jaw-dropped in their initial response. After voicing their general approval one partier exclaimed, "I guess you can't drink with us!" I laughed and explained that it wasn't an issue of "can't," but that I didn't need to drink with them. I didn't have a desire to drink with them. I shared the words in the Bible where the apostle Paul wrote, "...and do not be drunk with wine, for that is dissipation, but be filled with the Spirit."[70] I boldly shared that their drunkenness was a counterfeit for something that God wanted them to experience: the filling of the Holy Spirit.

Drug and alcohol abuse are clear counterfeits of what God intends for you and me, and they are not even "supernote" quality fakes when compared with the real thing. I heard it said by a former drug abuser, "I never knew anyone who continued to use drugs and their life got better." I couldn't think of a better statement that could be made on the subject. If you have never been around drug and alcohol abusers and addicts, then you might not understand it. If your only view into the world of drugs and alcohol is from television, movies and music, then you likely have gotten the wrong impression. If you do not know real life from what is being counterfeited, you are a likely target for getting duped.

The portrayal of drugs and alcohol in popular media paints a picture of people having fun, gaining popularity, making more friends, getting positive attention, finding approval among peers and generally making life more interesting and tolerable. There is also the common misunderstanding that they are a solution to problems in life, when in reality they only create more serious problems. Rarely do you see the true picture. Instead of a snapshot of reality, you are given a Photoshop version that is edited to portray what is deemed to be desirable. Substance abuse destroys lives. The statistics on how many drunk driving deaths, drug overdoses, and related violent crimes occur each

---

[70] Ephesians 5:18

year fall short of the overwhelming desolation caused by it. It would be difficult to list all of the statistics necessary to give the full story. Stories of children's lives left in the wake. Stories of physical and sexual abuse. Stories of families torn apart by lies, theft, poverty, violence, rape, insanity, prison, betrayal and an unfortunate list of many other heartbreaking effects on account of drugs abuse and drunkenness.

I carry the regret of having walked that road for a short while, but I have also had the privilege of spending the last twenty years of my life ministering in a variety of places and situations, including the streets of Chicago, prisons, jails, juvenile centers, and youth groups. All of them are places you will encounter the ferocity and insidiousness of substance abuse. I also have friends whose lives have been affected; some in prison or jail, one who committed suicide and several who have left their families. All of them have paid much too high of a price for their addictions, yet remain trapped in a desperate bondage that, short of a miracle, they will never escape.

I have as many friends, if not more, who have escaped the counterfeit life of drugs and alcohol and have found hope, deliverance and purpose in Jesus Christ. This miracle has not been kept secret; it just doesn't happen to be popular on network television or in Hollywood flicks. The answer was not found in a rule that says, "... and do not be drunk with wine..." but in a promise that says, "...but be filled with the Spirit..."[71] I cannot adequately describe what a miracle it is to have the unmerited privilege of being filled with the Spirit of God. It is the promise for those who have surrendered their lives to Him, "...do you not

---

[71] Ephesians 5:18

know that your body is a temple of the Holy Spirit?"[72] I can tell you firsthand that my drug use in the past had left me empty and desperate. On the other hand, I also know what it is like to have received God's Spirit into my life by becoming a child of His through faith in Jesus Christ. He has completely satisfied my heart, soul and mind. The emptiness I had once experienced has been filled forever.

Whether you realize it or not, any unfulfilled longing deep down inside of you has its fulfillment through the Spirit of God saturating your life. Don't fall for a counterfeit and don't rest until you have found the destiny that God has prepared for you.

---

[72] 1 Corinthians 6:19a

## Scriptures for Chapter 23

"And do not get drunk with
wine, for that is dissipation, but
be filled with the Spirit."

### Ephesians 5:18

"Peter said to them, 'Repent, and
each of you be baptized in the name
of Jesus Christ for the forgiveness of
your sins; and you will receive the
gift of the Holy Spirit.'"

### Acts 2:38

"Now the deeds of the flesh
are evident, which are... envying,
drunkenness, carousing, and things
like these, of which I forewarn you,
just as I have forewarned you, that
those who practice such things will
not inherit the kingdom of God."

### Galatians 5:19a, 21

# Chapter 24: Never Enough

In the classic Dr. Suess book, "How the Grinch Stole Christmas," the sinister and bitter Mr. Grinch thinks that by stealing all of the Whos' Christmas presents he will ruin Christmas for Who-ville. His plan backfires when the Whos celebrate Christmas together with joy and peace in spite of the missing gifts, which perplexes the Grinch and softens his heart. What would be the response of our society today if we woke up one morning and found that all of our stuff was gone? I really doubt that there would be songs of peace and joy; probably more along the lines of what the Grinch was expecting. Worse yet, shouts of anger and rage. The retaliation could really get ugly.

It is not unusual to find some general concern about sex, violence and drugs in today's media but there's another big one, maybe even the biggest, that has snuck past unnoticed or worse yet, intentionally ignored. It is the marketing of discontentment. The goal is to make you feel that you need a new look, a new car, a new TV, a new smartphone, a new house, a new spouse, a new chair, a new light bulb, a new diet, a new game, a new attitude, and so on. Why? So that you'll be happy and fulfilled? Not really. They market it so that you will buy products and ideas that will ultimately line their corporate wallets with cash, while they pitch the idea that you will finally be happy and your life will be better.

Does happiness come from money, possessions, makeovers, upgrades, new gadgets and shiny trinkets? It really doesn't, and even though the corporations may truly think that their product will make you happy, they are also working hard to create the next cool product that will make you feel like you are missing out on something if you don't have it. The tragedy is not that we have bought the products, but rather that we have bought into the deception of equating a better life and happiness with having more stuff. We have embraced the world's views about money, status, and possessions as the roads to a better life. Before we could be taken hostage with this direction of thinking, we first had to be lured by an even greater lie: that life is about pursuing a personal road of happiness and a better life than what we currently have. Jesus is not against happiness or progress in our lives, but His definitions are taken from a different dictionary than ours.

I could hardly expect a generation without Christ to be concerned about this, but for those longing to follow Jesus, we must stop at nothing to walk in His steps and adopt the same set of definitions about what makes life better and what brings happiness. "...Beware, and be on your guard against every form of greed; for not even when one has an abundance does his life consist of his possessions."[73] – Jesus

The following teaching by Jesus is His definition of happiness. He doesn't call it happiness in our sense of the word, but brings out something much deeper. Happiness is merely an emotion that comes and goes but the concept of being blessed is where the depth of true "happiness" is found.

"Blessed are the poor in spirit for theirs is the kingdom of heaven. Blessed are those who mourn for they shall be comforted. Blessed are the gentle for they shall inherit the

---

[73] Luke 12:15

earth. Blessed are those who hunger and thirst for righteousness for they shall be satisfied. Blessed are the merciful for they shall receive mercy. Blessed are the pure in heart, for they shall see God. Blessed are the peacemakers for they shall be called sons of God. Blessed are those who have been persecuted for the sake of righteousness for theirs is the kingdom of heaven. Blessed are you when people insult you and persecute you, and falsely say all kinds of evil against you because of Me. Rejoice and be glad, for your reward in heaven is great; for in the same way they persecuted the prophets who were before you." – Jesus[74]

There is a steady pulse in media that is coming from the heart of a society whose lust for money, power, notoriety, and possessions is never satisfied. This has sadly infiltrated the lives of many who say they are followers of Jesus. Yet how can we follow two separate roads that go in different directions?

"No one can serve two masters; for either he will hate the one and love the other, or he will be devoted to one and despise the other. You cannot serve God and wealth." [75]
– Jesus

"For the love of money is a root of all sorts of evil, and some by longing for it have wandered away from the faith and pierced themselves with many griefs."[76]

---

[74] Matthew 5:3-12
[75] Matthew 6:24
[76] 1 Timothy 6:10

"But the worries of the world, and the deceitfulness of riches, and the desires for other things enter in and choke the word, and it becomes unfruitful."[77] – Jesus

What exactly does it take to follow Jesus when it comes to money and possessions? One medium-sized word and one gigantic concept that continues to be voluntarily neglected: contentment. Contentment simply means being satisfied with what you have.

"Make sure that your character is free from the love of money, being content with what you have; for He Himself has said, "I will never desert you, nor will I ever forsake you."[78]

"But godliness actually is a means of great gain when accompanied by contentment. For we have brought nothing into the world, so we cannot take anything out of it either. If we have food and covering, with these we shall be content. But those who want to get rich fall into temptation and a snare and many foolish and harmful desires which plunge men into ruin and destruction."[79]

"For I have learned to be content in whatever circumstances I am. I know how to get along with humble means, and I also know how to live in prosperity; in any and every circumstance I have learned the secret of being filled and

---

[77] Mark 4:19

[78] Hebrews 13:5

[79] 1 Timothy 6:6-9

going hungry, both of having abundance and suffering need. I can do all things through Him who strengthens me."[80]

The Bible has a lot to say on this subject because it is hardly a new one. We are dealing with a compound problem of affluence in our society topped with an unhealthy dose of being spoiled, greedy, ungrateful and proud of it.

The total U.S. teen spending for a single year (products bought by and for teens) is $258.7 billion.[81] Teens have become a huge target for corporations to reach. The result is an overwhelming barrage of advertising that wants to get teens' attention no matter what. They are not just pitching a new look, a smartphone, or a new band that's on the block; they are selling ideas, attitudes towards money and possessions, impressions about popularity and acceptance among peers. They will stop at nothing within the current legal bounds (and even that is debatable) to draw the interest and loyalty of this lucrative pool of big spenders. That is the reality we face and it is not only ugly, but it has become increasingly hard for those who wish to emulate Christ to escape its tenacious grip.

There is no excuse for any of us to just give in to the system no matter how pervasive it has become. The late G.K. Chesterton once said, "The Christian ideal has not been tried and found wanting; it has been found difficult and left untried." Our problem is not that it is impossible to follow Christ and live our lives with contentment; the problem is that we are unwilling to venture along that narrow path.

---

[80] Philippians 4:11b-13

[81] statisticbrain.com "Teen Consumer Spending Statistics"

## Scriptures for Chapter 24

"Therefore consider the
members of your earthly body
as dead to immorality, impurity,
passion, evil desire, and greed,
which amounts to idolatry."

### Colossians 3:5

"You shall not covet your
neighbor's house; you shall not
covet your neighbor's wife or his
male servant or his female servant
or his ox or his donkey or anything
that belongs to your neighbor."

### Exodus 20:17

"The seed which fell among the
thorns, these are the ones who have
heard, and as they go on their way
they are choked  with worries and
riches and pleasures of this life, and
bring no fruit to maturity." –Jesus

### Luke 8:14

## Chapter 25: Pneumatic Tubes for Store Wagons

Not far from where I used to live there is something called the "Family Museum." The first time I saw a sign advertising it along the highway I laughed to myself while satirically thinking, "Families are so rare now that you can only find them in museums." It is actually a place for children to learn through activities and exhibits, but the pervading erosion of families today suggests that my jest may not be a far cry from reality.

So much has changed in the last 100 years. A women's magazine in 1900 printed some predictions for the year 2000. Some of their ideas were really close;

"Automobiles will be cheaper than horses are today."

"Hot or cold air will be turned on from spigots to regulate the temperature of a house as we now turn on hot or cold water from spigots to regulate the temperature of a bath."

"Man will see around the world. Persons and things of all kinds will be brought within focus of cameras connected electronically with screens at the opposite ends of circuits, thousands of miles at a span."

"Wireless telephone and telegraph circuits will span the world."

"Photographs will be telegraphed from any distance..."

"Grand Opera will be telephoned to private homes, and will sound as harmonious as though enjoyed from a theater box."

"Pneumatic tubes, instead of store wagons, will deliver packages and bundles."

Well, they sort of missed it on that last one, but what amazing insight they had. I'm sure many readers just baulked at the seemingly impossible predictions. Who would have predicted our current state of the family? Would they have guessed that over half of new marriages would end in divorce? Would they have envisioned the disconnected nature of the typical modern family? Would the lifestyles and actions of the fathers, mothers, teens, tweens and children have shocked them beyond belief? Could they foresee deadbeat dads, impoverished single moms, pervasive rebellion among teenagers, sexually active preteens and latchkey kids? Was there a foreboding of abortion on demand, partial birth abortion, rampant sexually transmitted disease, celebrated homosexuality, euthanasia, and school shootings?

The fallout from the breakdown of the family is a much larger topic than I can treat with justice in one chapter, so I will narrow this down a little more: the breakdown of relationships between parents and adolescents. Teens today live in a predominately peer based culture. It is not a society that they personally created; it is one that they have been born into and initiated into by default. Teens become their own sub-culture. Previously I have discussed the nature of marketing today and, believe it or not, the common struggle between parents and teens is a careful and strategic campaign being marketed through popular teen media.

"Often there's a kind of official and systematic rebelliousness that's reflected in media products pitched at kids. It's part of the official rock video worldview. It's part of the official advertising worldview that your parents are creeps, teachers are nerds and idiots, authority figures are laughable, nobody can really understand kids except the corporate sponsor. That huge authority has, interestingly enough, emerged as the sort of tacit superhero of consumer culture. That's the coolest entity of all."[82]

– Mark Crispin-Miller

Many families today have recognized the battle facing them, and are fighting to capture and keep the hearts of their children. The family is God's invention and when it follows the Maker's directions, it works accordingly. For the young readers of this book, you need to know that God is not entertained by teenage rebellion; hear what He had to say to the nation of Israel concerning it:

"If any man has a stubborn and rebellious son who will not obey his father or his mother, and when they chastise him, he will not even listen to them, then his father and mother shall seize him, and bring him out to the elders of his city at the gateway of his hometown. They shall say to the elders of his city, 'This son of ours is stubborn and rebellious, he will not obey us, he is a glutton and a drunkard.' Then all the men of

---

[82] Communications Professor, NYU (quoted on PBS Frontline: Merchants of Cool)

his city shall stone him to death; so you shall remove the evil from your midst, and all Israel will hear of it and fear."[83]

God was not joking around. I have a strong feeling that He would have some strong words to say about MTV and any other forms of media that glamorize, promote and endorse rebellion.

I have some more personal confessions to make about my years as an adolescent. I was very rebellious towards my parents and other authority figures. I had an unreasonable bitterness towards my dad from a young age that drove a wedge between us. There were times that I let my guard down, but it wasn't until I surrendered my life to Christ that I really began to respect my dad in a God honoring way. Again, this area of my life was pointed in its proper direction once I finally turned my eyes to Jesus and took them off of the world.

Families may not be "cool" according to the definition coming from contemporary culture, but they are needed. Each one of us must follow Christ as a member of a family, according to His instructions, not popular culture. The Bible gives clear instructions for fathers, mothers, children, elderly, bosses and employees. Have you made it a point to find out what the Bible says for your current role in the family?

Don't buy into media's portrayal of family. Instead, fulfill your unique role with honor and integrity. No doubt many of you reading this live in less than ideal family situations. Some are filled with conflict, distrust, betrayal, rejection or seemingly lesser things like disinterest, emotional distance or favoritism. We can't always control our circumstances but we can follow the example of Christ, with God's help, and live a life of love as our

---

[83] Deuteronomy 21:18-21

goal and motivation. We can rise above our temporary conflicts and troubles to reflect the light of Christ in our homes. The peer based culture might be dominant in society, but it does not have to dominate your life.

Parents have always had their challenges raising children prior to the digital age. The plethora of technologies and entertainment options has made the role of a parent exponentially more difficult. When it comes to media regulations, there are several different categories that parents and teens might fall into. Ideally, there is the concerned, protective and loving family that puts into practice the Biblical principles of discernment regarding media, with the children respecting the guidelines. The best chance of this working is when there is a strong relationship between the parents and children, where household rules are taught in the context of love for God and each other.

Some teens live in homes that have a commitment to honor God, and that may create tension when the child wants to be "in the know" and relate with peers concerning pop culture. Parents need to lovingly hold their ground and teens need to respect the rules of the home. It may sound old fashioned, but it's true and Biblical.

A home cannot function properly without this guidance. The purpose is to train the heart to make wise choices. God gave Israel the Law, but His ultimate goal was to transform lives by writing the law upon our hearts. The apostle Paul wrote, "The law is not made for a righteous person, but for the lawless and insubordinate, for the ungodly and for sinners..."[84] The Apostle

---

[84] 1 Timothy 1:9

John wrote "Sin is lawlessness..."[85]  Until the heart is changed by the Spirit of God it cannot be without law.  Children need to be taught that rules are not the ultimate goal, but a changed heart that has the rules written inside. Until that happens a person must be governed by external guidelines. "Therefore the Law has become our tutor to lead us to Christ, so that we may be justified by faith. But now that faith has come, we are no longer under a tutor."[86]

On the other end of the spectrum is the home that has no restrictions on media other than what is not accessible. According to research by the Kaiser Family Foundation only 3 in 10 young people between the ages of 8 and 18 have any rules about how much time they can spend watching TV, playing video games, or using a computer. This can stem from the absence of parents in the lives of their children or from a conflict born in the past. Many adults today had conflicts with their parents during their teens over music and movies.  They felt they were misunderstood, treated unjustly or simply subjected to old fashioned views, and in many cases vowed not to impose the same restrictions on their own children someday. Right or wrong in their assessment, they kept true to that vow and have either set very loose regulations, or have given their children free reign with media selections and invested time.

In the middle are various elements of both extremes.  If there is not a strong family bond, media can be a volatile issue in the home. Without proper love, nurture and care, teens can become bitter about any restrictions because their peers live with different household standards. These are youth who usually can't

---

[85] 1 John 3:4

[86] Galatians 3:24-25

wait to get out of the house temporarily or even permanently in order to indulge in media that is contraband at home. In this case the real issue is not media but family relationships. If you are a parent, you might choose to battle it out, but you might lose the war if you lose your child's heart along the way. This is not a book about parenting, so if this describes your family situation I hope you will seek further help which is readily accessible.

Parents provide accountability that peers do not in most cases. It's a very important factor that God has naturally built into the home to give young people time to gain wisdom and understanding before venturing out into the world unguarded.

The accountability factor is very obvious when interacting with young people. If you are a teen you need your parent's guidance. If you are a parent reading this book, your children desperately need your guidance, your presence, your concern, your love.

My heart breaks over what I hear professing Christian youth laughing at today. They have been trained to laugh at heartbreaking realities by being desensitized through their steady diet of entertainment. I can say with certainty that God is not laughing. His own heart is not unmoved by the tragic consequences of a generation that laughs at things that are wicked, reprobate, and heartless.

If accountability is not found in the home, it would be great if a young person could find it among their peers or adults in their church. Unfortunately, it seems to be a rare thing to find accountability for media use among people in the church. I couldn't tell you how many times I've encountered the following scenario when speaking at youth groups:

The night begins with a welcome from the youth pastor and a few pertinent announcements followed by a time of singing.

The youth group joins in a seemingly genuine time of worship and passionate praise songs, declaring love for Jesus and singing about dedication to following Him. They are often anthems of obedience, devotion and zeal, which is very moving and spiritual looking. After a prayer and an introduction, I am invited to speak. Since the topic is media and I am unsure whether this youth group is as steeped in contemporary entertainment as much as the average, I proceed with a brief poll by having them show a raise of hands for various media questions. I discover that the majority of them watch raunchy rated R movies, play ultra-violent video games and they rattle off names of their favorite musicians and groups whose songs are full of obscene lyrics. Hardly what I would call keeping each other accountable.

In the United States we have over a half million churches, and thousands of Christian bookstores and radio stations. Plus we have numerous Christian television programs, Christian schools, Christian colleges and seminaries. There is no shortage of Christian teaching resources, gimmick driven Bible studies, Christian software, Christian clothing, Christian board games and even Christian breath mints. What we don't have is an abundance of obedience to God and to His word. Don't fall for the counterfeit. Life to the fullest is not defined by an absence of parental authority or through unnecessary culture-driven conflict.

## Scriptures for Chapter 25

"But realize this, that in the last days difficult times will come. For men will be lovers of self, lovers of money, boastful, arrogant, revilers, disobedient to parents, ungrateful, unholy..."

**2 Timothy 3:1-2**

"Children, obey your parents in the Lord, for this is right.

"Honor your father and mother (which is the first commandment with a promise), so that it may be well with you, and that you may live long on the earth.

"Fathers, do not provoke your children to anger, but bring them up in the discipline and instruction of the Lord."

**Ephesians 6:1-4**

## Chapter 26: Red Hair and Blue Skin

She thought it was a curse to be endowed with red hair and such sensitive milky white skin. In fact, her skin was so white that her veins gave it a blue tint. Though some people coveted such a look, Rachel despised her genetic makeup. She wanted to have the bronze sunbaked look of her peers who spent much of their time on the sunny Southern California beaches. She learned the hard way that her desires came with a great price as she had endured sunburn after sunburn. Blisters, sunspots, and itchy peeling skin remained the consequences of overexposure to the sun's radiation.

Today, Rachel's attitude was different for a change. A close friend of the family, who was several years older than Rachel, had just found out that the growing abnormal spot on her shoulder was malignant. Emily had spent much of her young life on the same beaches soaking in the same sunshine and ultraviolet rays, and now her body was paying the price. Rachel thought it was so unfair for her friend to be going through the frightening ordeal of cancer, even though the doctor had given her a very hopeful prognosis for treatment and recovery. Emily would have to be much more careful from now on with her body. Rachel walked along the beach that day contemplating her childish woes with a wide brimmed sun hat and her blue skin lathered in sunscreen.

Many people today expose themselves to spiritually and morally harmful ideas and images through their media choices because they do not hold any convictions otherwise. Do you remember the definition of conviction that I gave at the beginning of this book? A conviction is something you believe so strongly that it will guide your actions even when under pressure. If you do not believe that your media choices have an influence on the life you live, the way you think and the decisions you make, then you probably won't concern yourself with developing convictions about the matter. At least not until you begin to suffer the consequences of your actions due to a lack of convictions.

Encouraging you to develop strong or stronger convictions about your media intake will not necessarily cure you of any existing "cancer" due to previous exposure. There are many types of spiritual and moral cancers in our lives that need special treatment. Even if you were to never see another movie, watch another television show, listen to another song, play another video game, view another web site or read another magazine or book, you would still be plagued with the existing cancer. Are you struggling with hate, anger or violent thoughts? What about depression, despair, suicidal thoughts or self-mutilation? Are you trapped in lust, pornography or other sexual activities? Are you trying to escape or drown out your problems with drugs or alcohol? Does your view of success revolve around money, status or power? All of these things and more can be fueled by your media consumption. Merely avoiding potentially harmful influences will not cure the problems any more than avoiding the sun would cure a case of skin cancer. You cannot passively recover on your own. You need a doctor to remove the destructive nature of the disease from your life. Once that is taken care of, it should become obvious to avoid those things which fuel the areas in your life that keep you from living the life that God has planned for you.

Jesus said that He was the great physician who came to heal those who were sick. In order to live life to its fullest, the road to recovery must begin with Him. If you recognize that you need the power of Jesus to bring spiritual, moral or physical healing to your life, and you have never truly made a decision to go to Him for help, don't hesitate any longer. His office is always open and there is no wait time.

"For the Scripture says, 'Whoever believes in Him will not be disappointed.'"[87]

"The Lord is near to all who call upon Him, to all who call upon Him in truth."[88]

"I shall lift up the cup of salvation and call upon the name of the Lord."[89]

"And having been made perfect, He became to all those who obey Him the source of eternal salvation."[90]

You don't have to have it all together to approach God, but you have to believe He is able to save you. Calling upon the Lord in prayer is an act of faith. You don't have to have the right words to say, just let Him know that you need Him. Pour out your heart and soul to the God who loves you and wants to hear from you. He promises that you won't be disappointed.

---

[87] Romans 10:11

[88] Psalm 145:18

[89] Psalm 116:13

[90] Hebrews 5:9

## Scriptures for Chapter 26

"Therefore if you have been raised up with Christ, keep seeking the things above, where Christ is, seated at the right hand of God. Set your mind on the things above, not on the things that are on earth. For you have died and your life is hidden with Christ in God. When Christ, who is our life, is revealed, then you also will be revealed with Him in glory."

### Colossians 3:1-4

"But flee from these things, you man of God, and pursue righteousness, godliness, faith, love, perseverance and gentleness."

### 1 Timothy 6:11

"Let us draw near with a sincere heart in full assurance of faith, having our hearts sprinkled clean from an evil conscience and our bodies washed with pure water."

### Hebrews 10:22

## Chapter 27: The Battle is not Against Hollywood

The night seemed like so many others in the weeks leading up to Christmas. Who would have known it was actually leading up to war. America had a rude awakening on the morning of December 7th, 1941, when Japanese aircraft began a deadly attack on a fleet of U.S. ships that were moored at Pearl Harbor on the Island of Oahu, Hawaii. Two hours later there were 2,403 serviceman and civilians dead, 1,178 injured and an entire nation in shock and incensed. The Japanese had temporarily succeeded in their goal to cripple the U.S. Pacific Fleet in order to secure an advantage on their invasion of Southeast Asia. Five battleships had been sunk, sixteen more were damaged and 188 aircraft were destroyed in the attack. At 1:10 p.m. the next day, our nation's representatives voted 388 to 1 in favor of declaring war on Japan.

One of the many intriguing stories about this surprise attack is that there appears to have been many warnings that were not taken seriously enough. There was a critical Japanese message that was intercepted on December 6th that revealed an imminent attack, but the entire message was not completely decoded and interpreted until the morning of December 7th. Due to a temporary loss of radio contact with Hawaii, an alert was sent by telegraph, and because of delays, did not arrive in Oahu until four hours after the attack had begun. On the Island itself, an Army radar operator had sighted over fifty incoming planes, but his report was misinterpreted by superiors. Likewise, the report of a submarine that was spotted and sunk outside of the harbor by a U.S. destroyer just prior to the aerial attack was not given due attention or gravity. Pearl Harbor had not been on a state of alert because, at this time, America did not anticipate an attack from Japan prior to a declaration of war.

Today's media is more than just the world's billboard to advertise its ideas and sell its products, it is also a very large part of the enemy's artillery against the Kingdom of God. The Bible tells us that our battle is not against flesh and blood, but against the spiritual forces of wickedness in the heavenly places. I will not beat around the bush on this one; you cannot spiritually afford to be ignorant of the tactics and weapons of the enemy. If you are too "enlightened" to believe in such realities as Satan, and demons, and a spiritual war that is waging for the souls of mankind, then you are likely going to get caught by surprise. God has made it very clear to us that this unseen battle is real and the consequences are eternal. We have been given sufficient warning. The Bible also states that in the end, God wins this war, but that doesn't mean lives are not lost or that every battle is won along the way. I hope to bring a greater awareness of this particular battle line called entertainment, as well as encourage you to join the fight and be prepared.

An enemy in war is looking for weakness; holes in defense, lack of tight security, confused intelligence data or anything else that can help gain an upper hand. "Be of sober spirit, be on the alert. Your adversary, the devil, prowls about like a roaring lion, seeking someone to devour. But resist him, firm in your faith."[91] Have you ever watched a documentary about lions in the wild? If so, you've probably learned already that they don't like fast food. They have to hunt for their dinner, and it's not really

---

[91] 1 Peter 5:8-9a

advantageous when hunting to spend all the time and energy chasing fast and healthy wildebeest, so they often look for weakness. They prey upon an old, slow one, or an inexperienced young one, or an animal that is crippled. Why not go for the easy target? Besides that, they nearly always attempt to take their victim by surprise.

Likewise, Satan doesn't just pop into your room, emerging from a puff of smoke in a red suit with horns on his head and a pitchfork in hand, and kindly ask you if you don't mind if he destroys your life and takes you to hell with him someday. You would probably tell him to get lost. The Bible says "...and no wonder, for even Satan disguises himself as an angel of light."[92] He wants to appear as the good guy. "He was a murderer from the beginning, and does not stand in the truth, because there is no truth in him. Whenever he speaks a lie, he speaks from his own nature; for he is a liar and the father of lies."[93]

The Bible describes the enemy not only as a prowling lion and the father of lies, but also as a tempter and an accuser. Once in a while he appears on the scene like he did when tempting Eve in the Garden of Eden, or when Jesus was in the wilderness, fasting for forty days just prior to the beginning of His public ministry. Yet, the general portrayal of him is as an unseen perpetrator of lies as well as an invisible instigator of spiritual trouble. "Put on the full armor of God that you may be able to stand against the schemes of the devil."[94] The apostle Paul wrote to the Corinthian church and asserted a general awareness among them of the enemy's tactics, "...so that no advantage would be

---

[92] 2 Corinthians 11:14

[93] John 8:44b

[94] Ephesians 6:11

taken of us by Satan, for we are not ignorant of his schemes."[95] That verse describes the alertness of the church back then, but it doesn't necessarily describe the state of the church today.

The church today appears to be ignorant of his schemes, especially concerning his intense propaganda campaign found in media. So many have embraced nearly every form of entertainment without restraint or wisdom or discernment. Simply recognizing his arsenal is a good start for waging spiritual war.

If you are going to stand against his schemes, you need a good defense, a good offense and a willingness to fight to the end. One of the most powerful verses on spiritual warfare is found in James 4:7, "Submit therefore to God, resist the devil and he will flee from you." There is no hope of successful resistance to the powers of darkness if you have not embraced The Light. Flashlights are pretty common but have you ever heard of a flashdark? There's no such thing on the market because darkness is only the absence of light, but light is a very real thing. A very small light can accomplish a lot in pitch blackness but there is no contraption that can send a beam of darkness. "This is the message we have heard from Him and announce to you, that God is Light, and in Him there is no darkness at all."[96] The one who wishes to survive in this spiritual war must first "submit to God" before making an attempt to resist the devil. The enemy is not ignorant of Scripture. We can assume that he is scheming to keep people from their one sure defense, submission to God.

---

[95] 2 Corinthians 2:11
[96] 1 John 1:5

How can the enemy keep someone from submitting themselves to God? One way is to take them captive or captivate them. What is our generation captivated with? What are you captivated with? You will submit yourself to whatever or whoever it is you are attracted to and it will eventually encompass every area of your life. The enemy's deceptions are attractive, stimulating, addictive, and spiritually deadly. On the other end of the spectrum, following God can be difficult, narrow, and painful. Let's not forget that following God is rewarded with an eternity with Him, in the light of His glory, in unimagined wonder. "But just as it is written, 'Things which eye has not seen and ear has not heard, and which have not entered the heart of man, all that God has prepared for those who love Him.'"[97] If your life is captivated merely by temporary things, you might have eternity to regret it; but if you are captivated with God, then the difficulties of your short life on earth will vanish like a shadow in the light of eternity.

In this spiritual struggle we are given further instructions in the Bible about our defense and offense that we cannot ignore.

"For our struggle is not against flesh and blood, but against the rulers, against the powers, against the world forces of this darkness, against the spiritual forces of wickedness in the heavenly places. Therefore, take up the full armor of God, that you may be able to resist in the evil day, and having done everything, to stand firm. Stand firm therefore, having girded your loins with the truth, and having put on the breastplate of righteousness and having shod your feet with the preparation of the gospel of peace. In addition to all,

---

[97] 1 Corinthians 2:9

taking up the shield of faith with which you will be able to extinguish all the flaming missiles of the evil one. And take the helmet of salvation and the sword of the Spirit, which is the word of God, with prayer and petition pray at all times in the Spirit, and with this in view, be on the alert  with all perseverance and petition for all the saints."[98]

You will never know what Jesus did or didn't do if you remain unfamiliar with the Word of God. The Scriptures say of themselves that it is a sword to wield in battle. When Jesus was tempted in the desert, Satan used Scripture out of context to try to tempt Jesus, but our Lord fought back with Scripture in its right context. Satan has taken the words of God and twisted them from the very beginning, and unless you are more than casually aware of God's Word, you will be at risk for getting caught in a trap and captivated. As a new Christian I made it a point to not read another book until I had first read the entire Bible. Even now I will prioritize reading Scripture over other books. Not that other books cannot be helpful; I am hoping this one will be, but this, or any other book, cannot be an effective sword against the enemy. The Bible is not merely another book. All other books and forms of media must be subject to its righteous scrutiny.

Another important aspect of spiritual battle was mentioned as well in Ephesians 6—prayer. The Bible is full of teaching on prayer, so if you follow the above instructions, you will be taught better on the subject than I could accomplish here. If you want to help others on the Lord's side, there is nothing greater than prayer "...be on the alert with all perseverance and petition for all the saints." This ministry was inspired and cultivated

---

[98] Ephesians 6:12-18

through personal times of prayer, especially during the years that I was a full-time youth pastor. I would get the current issue of "Plugged In" magazine, which provides reviews and commentary on popular entertainment, and my heart would break as I would read about all the different messages being marketed to this generation. I felt helpless to make a difference until pouring out my heart in prayer for our generation, that we would recognize the enemy's plot and would turn from his captivating facade to follow the true life found in Jesus Christ.

Another reality you may face in this spiritual war is that you may not have much company in the trenches. Not only that, it is likely you will encounter rejection, misunderstanding, accusations, confrontations and criticisms from your peers and sometimes from your family.

"If the world hates you, you know that it has hated Me before it hated you. If you were of the world, the world would love its own; but because you are not of the world, but I chose you out of the world, because of this the world hates you."[99] – Jesus

"Blessed are you when men hate you, and ostracize you, and insult you, and scorn your name as evil, for the sake of the Son of Man."[100] – Jesus

---

[99] John 15:18-19
[100] Luke 6:22

"You will be hated by all because of My name, but it is the one who has endured to the end who will be saved."[101]
– Jesus

One more aspect on this subject of spiritual war is the question, "What do you defend?" What you defend speaks a lot about who you are and what matters most to you. I have encountered young people and adults who defend their favorite TV show, favorite band, favorite website, favorite movie, favorite actor or actress, favorite video game, and other media. It is rare to find a young person or adult today who are willing and ready to defend the gospel of Jesus Christ in a lost world.

Don't give in or give up! Jesus is the One we are following and He has promised to never leave us or forsake us.

---

[101] Matthew 10:22

## Scriptures for Chapter 27

"...and they may come to their senses and escape from the snare of the devil, having been held captive by him to do his will."

### 2 Timothy 2:26

"For the weapons of our warfare are not of the flesh, but divinely powerful for the destruction of fortresses. We are destroying speculations and every lofty thing raised up against the knowledge of God, and we are taking every thought captive to the obedience of Christ."

### 2 Corinthians 10:4-5

"See to it that no one takes you captive through philosophy and empty deception, according to the tradition of men, according to the elementary principles of the world, rather than according to Christ."

### Colossians 2:8

## Chapter 28: Robbing God

It was riveting to hear the personal story of a young man from Africa named Obang as he shared one evening at a church in our area. He had grown up in Ethiopia near the Sudan border in a region plagued with ethnic violence. When he was eleven years old, his life was turned upside down when the area came under attack while he was attending an elementary school in a neighboring village. The teachers ordered the class to the floor when they began to hear gunfire, but as the students cowered under desks, they sensed that something was terribly wrong when the surface of the floor started getting warmer. It didn't take long to realize that the school had been set on fire and they were soon to be engulfed in flames. Obang and a few others decided to make an escape attempt through a window and face a possible spray of bullets. It appeared that either way they would die. Only a few were willing to chance it and the rest no longer had that choice moments later when the room was overcome with flames.

The rest of the story was almost surreal as he hid from soldiers behind some rocks near a river, and waited until the violence had passed, only to wander home alone through the trail of carnage left by the attackers. When he arrived at his village, he found it decimated with the charred bodies of the villagers all over. When he didn't find anyone in his family, he joined a small group of survivors who were attempting a 1,300 mile trek to a refugee camp in Kenya.

After enduring difficult and dangerous terrain, crossing a crocodile infested river, and suffering with wounded feet and a lack of food, he finally made it to the refugee camp only to face five years of hardship, hunger and seeming hopelessness. Even though it was illegal to leave the camp, he had made several attempts to get to an American Embassy with the knowledge that they were providing homes in the U.S. for those in his situation. After being arrested a couple of times and sent back to the camp, he continued his quest and was finally able to get through, resulting in a one way ticket to America. By a miracle he soon discovered that one of his older brothers had also survived and was living in Minnesota.

The good news didn't stop there. After being reunited with his brother, the two later found out that the rest of their family had also survived and was still in Africa. When we heard him speak, he had yet to be able to visit them but had talked with them over the phone. He shared boldly how God had shown mercy to him, and how his faith had remained steady through the many intense trials. It might surprise you that the most remarkable thing he communicated had nothing to do with his native struggles; he truly believed that living as a Christian in America was more difficult with all of the distractions and affluence that he faced in contrast with his former troubles.

You and I could never gain Christ and the eternal life that He gives by obeying any list of do's and don'ts. The Scriptures make it very clear that a person can only receive Christ's gift of salvation through God's grace and by our faith. "For by grace you have been saved through faith, and that not of yourselves, it is a gift of God, not of works lest anyone should boast."[102] It

---

[102] Ephesians 2:8-9

couldn't be clearer in the Bible that we are not saved by doing good things and avoiding bad things. We can only be saved from our sins and the temporary and eternal consequences of those sins by simply believing that Jesus died on a cross that we might have eternal life. "For God so loved the world, that He gave His only begotten Son, that whoever believes in Him shall not perish, but have eternal life."[103] The problem many are facing today is that they have not understood the rest of the story. Let me quote Ephesians 2:10, which immediately follows the previous verse on salvation by grace and faith. It says, "For we are God's workmanship, created in Christ Jesus for good works that He has prepared beforehand that we should walk in them." In a nutshell this is telling us that we have a destiny.

Before you even knew who God was, He knew who you were and had a plan for your life. That plan involves "good works that He has prepared." It should be very exciting to know that there is a divine plan for your life, but there's a catch to this verse; it continues... "that we should walk in them." "Should" does not necessarily equal "will." God communicates to us that He has a plan that you should walk in, but unfortunately too many refuse to follow that plan, and in turn are missing out on what will truly make life most fulfilling: God's plan for you.

So many people today are afraid to follow God with all their heart, soul, mind and strength. They are afraid to allow God's word to speak to them about the choices they make. They are afraid to allow God's word to guide them concerning media habits. Why are they afraid? I believe they are afraid of missing out on something. If you have been seduced by entertainment's idea of life to the fullest, then you might feel that you would be

---

[103] John 3:16

robbed of some meaningful experience if you were to really obey and follow the Lord. Following Jesus might involve living differently from your peers, being made fun of or mocked, making different choices, having higher standards, and being rejected by friends and sometimes family. For many, that is too high of a price to pay because they think they might be missing out. Ultimately they are afraid that God intends to rob them of the fun years of their life, rob them of teenage pleasures, intimate friendships and shared cultural experiences. The sad reality is that they are only robbing themselves of life to its fullest and robbing God of the plans that He has prepared for their life.

"For I know the plans that I have for you," declares the Lord, "plans for welfare, and not calamity, to give you a future and a hope."[104] – God

God's plans for you are good and will be the key that unlocks the solution to the gnawing emptiness inside of you that longs for something more. That longing will find its fulfilment in the will of God.

---

[104] Jeremiah 29:11

## Scriptures for Chapter 28

"You shall love the Lord your God with all your heart and with all your soul and with all your might."

### Deuteronomy 6:5

"Only fear the Lord and serve Him in truth with all your heart; for consider what great things He has done for you."

### 1 Samuel 12:24

"Do not let your heart envy sinners, but live in the fear of the Lord always."

### Proverbs 23:17

"But whoever drinks of the water that I will give him shall never thirst; but the water that I will give him will become in  him a well of water springing up to eternal life." – Jesus

### John 4:14

## Chapter 29: The Power in Unplugging

It was a big adjustment when I moved to Chicago right out of high school. Among the many changes was a disappointing discovery that it was nearly impossible to see any stars at night. I had grown up in the country and spent many nights staring at the sky. I would gaze at the Milky Way, locate the Pleiades, point out the Northern Cross, watch Orion on the horizon, and catch sight of a meteorite. I even had the rare opportunity to see Halley's comet in 1986. In Chicago you were unlikely to see the moon unless it happened to be standing over your street.

Why couldn't I see the stars at night in Chicago? It is called light pollution. There are so many man-made lights in a city that it drowns out the view of the stars. They haven't gone away, but they are clouded by a blanket of artificial light. When you get out of the city and away from the lights, you can see the stars again. In the same way, we can see God clearer when there is not so much polluting our soul; "Blessed are the pure in heart for they shall see God."[105] The stars at night are not the only things in life that can seem to vanish. It reminds me of the times in my life when I think that God has disappeared. It's not that He isn't there; it's just that I don't see Him.

What keeps us from having a pure heart? One of the biggest factors is today's entertainment. The hours spent each day in front of various electronic screens can appear so harmless. Even the artificial lights in a city are welcome at night until you have a

---

[105] Matthew 5:8

desire to see the stars. Likewise, it is easy to get used to a constant stream of media until we realize that we are having trouble seeing God. Media pollution blocks out the light of God shining into our lives, and the person who longs for intimacy with Him must choose what is more important to them.

Have you ever struggled with your relationship with God in a similar way? Does He ever seem distant to you? Have you ever been uninspired in prayer or felt that reading the Bible was just a chore? Do you have the tendency to fill your life with noise because you are uneasy with silence? We are a generation that is addicted to entertainment and we don't know what to do with ourselves when it's quiet. Silence makes us nervous, and when we have leisure time with no plans, we tend to gravitate toward the TV, or a movie, or the internet out of habit. Do the things of the world seem much more attractive and interesting than the things of God?

Having spent many summers working at youth camps, I have often marveled at the impact they can have in the lives of young people. I have a good hunch that much of the effectiveness is due to the fact that the campers have to "unplug" from media for a few days. During that short time, the artificial light that has previously blocked their view begins to dissipate, and they begin to see God more clearly than before.

It is not that they haven't heard the same messages before at church, or in their homes. Often times the messages don't get through to the heart because it is experiencing a spiritual form of light pollution. If my hunch is right about the effectiveness of such a short break from media, imagine the growth we might experience if we began to "unplug" some of those distractions for longer periods of time. I'm convinced we will begin to see God more clearly.

What is a media fast? It means going without all or some portion of media for a set time in order to seek God. Do this as an individual or organize a group of participants to keep each other accountable. You will discover your cravings and how strong they are during this time, but it's not like fasting from food which your body actually needs. You don't physically need media in your life to survive. Thomas Edison didn't invent motion pictures with sound until 1913. The first television transmission was not until 1927 and the first regular broadcast was in 1936, both happening in England. Prior to that, society survived just fine and so will you if you take a break from it.

Be serious about the fast and use the time you would have spent on media to seek the Lord in prayer and Bible study. Take a real plunge and commit to 40 days at least. I promise you that you will live through it and likely emerge with a new perspective on life. Fast from whatever is most distracting in your life right now. Maybe it's television, or video games, or spending too much time on social media. It could mean putting the smartphone away for a while or turning off the radio at home or in your car. Whatever it might be, don't be a chicken. Learn what it means to pursue Christ at all costs.

"Then the king went off to his palace and spent the night fasting, and no entertainment was brought before him; and his sleep fled from him."[106]

"Abstain from every form of evil."[107]

---

[106] Daniel 6:18
[107] 1 Thessalonians 5:22

"Nevertheless, the firm foundation of God stands, having this seal, 'The Lord knows those who are His,' and, 'Everyone who names the name of the Lord is to abstain from wickedness.'"[108]

What are some of the media choices you make that might be distracting you from your relationship with God? Maybe it's time to consider switching from primetime to some quiet time.[109] From vegging out to crying out for wisdom.[110] From being taken captive to taking every thought captive.[111] From idol time (oops, I meant idle) to redeeming the time.[112] From the light pollution of the world to the authentic light of Christ.

---

[108] 2 Timothy 2:19

[109] Psalm 46:10

[110] Proverbs 8:1

[111] 2 Corinthians 10:5

[112] Ephesians 5:16

## Scriptures for Chapter 29

"Do not love the world nor the
things in the world.  If anyone
loves the world, the love of the
Father is not in him.  For all that
is in the world, the lust of the flesh
and the lust of the eyes and the
boastful pride of life, is not from the
Father, but is from the world.
The world is passing away, and
also its lusts; but the one who does
the will of God lives forever."

1 John 2:15-17

"But now you also, put them all aside:
anger, wrath, malice, slander, and
abusive speech from your mouth.
Do not lie to one another, since you
laid aside the old self with its evil
practices, and have put on the new
self who is being renewed to true
knowledge according to the image
of the One who created him."

Colossians 3:8-10

## Chapter 30: Boys, Snakes, and
## Insatiable Appetites

Camping trips were always a highlight of my boyhood and on one of these memorable outings I happened upon a baby bull snake. Like most boys, I was fascinated with snakes, toads, and lizards. I never hesitated trying to catch them, sometimes with success and sometimes not.

This little snake was an easy catch, though it was a little feisty once I nabbed it. The garter snakes I was used to catching were not as interesting as this one so I was determined to have it as a pet. Not knowing if Mom would approve, I decided not to trouble her over it and hid my new pet in an empty coffee can until I got home.

Once we were home, I moved my bully little snake into an aquarium that I placed in my closet. I wasn't sure what to feed him. I caught bugs and flies, but he didn't seem interested. The only thing he seemed to like was striking at me anytime I opened the lid to the tank. I ventured out on my bike to the public library and checked out a book on snakes. I wanted to find out what I should be feeding this aggressive little fiend that I hoped I could befriend through faithful care and provision.

When I got home, I found the section on bull snakes, but after comparing the picture of a baby bull snake with the one in my aquarium, I realized that it wasn't a match. What was it? I thumbed through the book looking for a positive identification and then I found it—a baby rattlesnake!

The picture and description matched: "Rattler babies have venom, short fangs and are dangerous from birth. In fact, they are more pugnacious than the adults. Although unable to make a rattling sound, the youngsters throw themselves into a defensive pose and strike repeatedly when disturbed." Without hesitation, I made an executive decision to let it go.

We need to be careful with what we let into our homes, whether it's poisonous snakes or troublesome entertainment habits. Danger doesn't always come with rattles. Sometimes the greatest threats are the ones that are not perceived as such. How many children are being raised from a young age with a steady stream of electronic media that fosters an insatiable appetite for more? These appetites are not satisfied during youth. The average age of a video game player in the U.S. is 31 years old, and 71 percent are age 18 or older.[113]

Many parents today don't see the harm of a generation of young boys growing up with a stunted purpose for life in the real world, while becoming accustomed to the unreal world of video games. Adventure is relegated to virtual goals and the false sense of accomplishment at the push of buttons and the flicker of pixels. Many of them can't play a real guitar and they don't know the real meaning of a hero. They think they can win battles and save the planet from invasion, but can they conquer the dishes in the kitchen or stave off the invasion of a counter-Biblical worldview into their own hearts and minds?

Many parents today don't believe that there's any harm in putting a TV in their toddler's bedroom. That's the case for 43% of 3 to 4 year olds in the U.S.[114] Did you know that one out of

---

[113] http://www.theesa.com/about-esa/industry-facts/

[114] http://www.medpagetoday.com/upload/2007/5/8/e1006.pdf

five children under the age of 3 has a TV in their bedroom? A TV doesn't appear to have fangs or rattles to some parents, yet according to a study published by the American Academy of Pediatrics (AAP):

"Sustained television viewing was associated with sleep, attention and aggressive behavior problems, and externalizing of problem behaviors. Concurrent television exposure was associated with fewer social skills. Having a television in the bedroom was associated with sleep problems and less emotional reactivity at age 5½."

The AAP recommended that children under two years old should not watch any TV and viewing should be very limited for children over two years old.

More importantly, how has this media revolution impacted the family? Has the family become stronger since the first color television broadcast in 1954? Have we given children a greater advantage over previous generations since the introduction of the first home video game console in 1972? With all the advantages of gaining information on the internet, have we accurately counted the cost when 90% of children between the ages of 8-16 have been exposed to pornography online (most of them while innocently doing homework)?

Electronic media in itself is not necessarily bad. Appropriate amusement in moderation is not an ominous danger. Not all snakes are poisonous. Yet our culture consistently demonstrates its tendency to be too careless about entertainment. Too careless about the insatiable appetites that are being fostered, too careless about the impact of content, too careless about the time being consumed, too careless about the long-term impact of convenient short-term diversions, and too careless about the wedge that is often being subtly driven between parents, children, siblings, and other relationships.

Some of entertainment's greatest dangers are the incessant forces that continue to foster the dismantling of families. A nasty brood of little venomous snakes that rob time, captivate hearts, diminish responsibilities, shirk accountability, sacrifice more important things, and neglect noble endeavors. They slither in and entice vicarious living, smug narcissism, a false sense of accomplishment, and unabashed escapism. The Bible says we are to be "…taking every thought captive to the obedience of Christ."[115] That doesn't mean making pets out of poisonous snakes.

---

[115] 2 Corinthians 10:5

## Scriptures for Chapter 30

"Now the deeds of the flesh are evident, which are: immorality, impurity, sensuality, idolatry, sorcery, enmities, strife, jealousy, outbursts of anger, disputes, dissensions, factions, envying, drunkenness, carousing, and things like these,

"Of which I forewarn you, just as I have forewarned you, that those who practice such things will not inherit the kingdom of God.

"But the fruit of the Spirit is love, joy, peace, patience, kindness, goodness, faithfulness, gentleness, self-control; against such things there is no law.

"Now those who belong to Christ Jesus have crucified the flesh with its passions and desires. If we live by the Spirit, let us also walk by the Spirit."

Galatians 5:19-25

## Chapter 31: It's All Fun and Games Until...

I am personally very squeamish about certain things, so I almost lost my lunch after reading an article in a magazine about a woodsman who was clearing land for a mining company and found himself in a mishap which left him pinned under a tree with a severely broken leg. After an hour of crying out for help, he gave up hope that anyone would hear him or come to look for him in time. Knowing his life could be at stake, he made a tourniquet using a shoestring and a wrench, and then used a pocket knife to amputate his own leg, cutting through the skin, muscle and fractured bone below his left knee. Then he dragged himself to his bulldozer and drove it a quarter of a mile to his truck. Having managed the manual transmission with his good leg, he drove over a mile until reaching the home of a farmer who called for help and took him from there to meet an ambulance on the way. He lived.

There is a similar true story that has been made into a movie about a climber who was alone and became pinned between some boulders. When he recognized his life was at stake, he chose to amputate his arm in order to save his own life. Nobody wants to lose a limb, but there comes a time when some people are forced to choose between losing a limb or losing their life.

Not every choice we make in life has such an extreme and apparent result, but every choice does have short-term and long-term effects on our lives. The common computer programming mantra says "garbage in, garbage out." The Bible says it this way

"Be not deceived; God is not mocked, for whatsoever a man soweth, that shall he also reap."[116]

According to research by the Kaiser Family Foundation, the average young person between the ages of 2 and 17 spends nearly six and a half hours a day in front of electronic screens which includes television, internet use and video games. Though some of the content being consumed might be harmless, the fact is that children and teens are being bombarded with images and messages about sex, drugs and alcohol, violence, hate and anger, depression, despair and suicide, greed, discontentment and a barrage of other things that are being stored in their hearts and minds. In a category all to itself is the worldview that has emerged and continues to saturate the bulk of youth culture concerning unbelief in absolute truth, as well as unfounded views about God and Christianity. As the garbage continues to go in, the statistics of spiritual, moral, and physical devastation continue to climb for this generation.

Only when a person comes to a place where honoring God and becoming like Jesus is more important to them than remaining electronically inebriated in the world of compromising entertainment, will they consider turning away from the things which pin them down spiritually and morally, to gain the freedom to experience real life.

When I was a sophomore in High School, a friend of mine used to come to my house and we would have BB gun wars. This was either before the days of paintball guns or at least before the days that we were aware of them. We did not wear goggles and had a minimum number of rules for our warfare.

---

[116] Galatians 6:7

We paid the price of our folly with welts and bruises, but we kept on with our antics.

During one such skirmish my friend was unreasonably upset with me, and recognizing the fire in his glare I made for cover behind a shed on our property. I wanted to spy out his position so I stealthily climbed up to the roof of the shed to peek over the ridge. Little did I know that he anticipated what I was up to and had a wicked plan to shoot me in the forehead as a joke. I heard the whizzing sound and found myself writhing in pain on the ground a moment later after the small ball of steel penetrated my right eye. I began to go into shock; I could not see out my eye and I was scared. It was a long night beginning with a trip to the ER and the removal of the BB from my eye. This was followed with excruciating pain, facing my parents, more excruciating pain, and wondering whether I would get my sight back (did I mention the excruciating pain?). I also listened to my father's gentle exhortation to me that God was trying to get my attention because of my continued wayward behavior. Excruciating pain has a way of getting our attention.

I did eventually get most of the sight back in my right eye, though it plagues me to this day. I could never imagine voluntarily gouging my own eye out if I thought it might help me stay on track with God. By some of the looks I get from people, you would think I had asked them to gouge an eye out when I suggest that it might be worth their while to regulate their media choices according to principles found in the Bible. Sometimes spiritual growth requires desperate measures.

Long before I began speaking and writing about the growing need for discernment and making wise media choices, Jesus said, "If your eye causes you to stumble, pluck it out and throw it from you. It is better for you to enter life with one eye, than to have two eyes and be cast into the fiery hell."[117] It may be time to clean house, time to rid your home of any toxic entertainment. You might be wondering, "How do I know what is toxic?" Would you be interested in a complete list? If so, you won't find one in this book, but there's an expert on the subject who can tell you exactly what toxic media needs to get out of the home. See footnote[118] for contact information.

To contact the world's leading expert on the identification of toxic media, speak to the Holy Spirit. He has a list for you, if you are willing to consult Him about the media in your home. The problem is that there are not many families or individuals willing to ask Him for wisdom and insight. Jesus wrote to seven churches in the book of Revelation and said to each of them, "He who has an ear, let him hear what the Spirit says to the churches."[119]

The personal steps that I have taken to pursue Christ could hardly come close to the type of sacrifice that Jesus called for in Matthew 18, yet I can relate to His message. I believe He has given us the ability to demonstrate self-control and develop God-honoring parameters to help us stay on track with His plan for us.

---

[117] Matthew 18:9

[118] The Holy Spirit

[119] Revelation 2:7, 2:11, 2:17, 2:29, 3:6, 3:13, 3:22

## Scriptures for Chapter 31

"I pray that the eyes of your heart may be enlightened, so that you will know what is the hope of His calling, what are the riches of the glory of His inheritance in the saints."

Ephesians 1:18

"If indeed you have heard Him and have been taught in Him, just as truth is in Jesus, that, in reference to your former manner of life, you lay aside the old self, which is being corrupted in accordance with the lusts of deceit,

"And that you be renewed in the spirit of your mind, and put on the new self, which in the likeness of God has been created in righteousness and holiness of the truth."

Ephesians 4:21-24

## Chapter 32: When East Should be West

Los Angeles traffic is notoriously bad. Navigating the labyrinth of highways is truly daunting for the stranger, which is a personal reference to myself based on experience. I was staying in L.A. for several weeks of ministry, and one of the invitations was to speak at a youth group in Valencia, about 45 minutes from Los Angeles in ideal traffic conditions—if there is such a thing in L.A.

The organizers of the meeting gave me meticulous directions, and guess what? They worked! I made it to the event with time to spare. Such was not the case on my return. I neglected to get step by step directions back to where I had started, and as I attempted to reverse navigate the directions I took one or more wrong exits without realizing it. Before long I had traversed even further from the city and discovered that something was amiss after seeing a road sign with distances to cities in Nevada!

I was heading the wrong direction. It was late and I was tired and frazzled. This was several years before owning a GPS or smartphone, so I considered my options. There were three possibilities.

You also have three options if you discover that you have taken a wrong turn in your life in the context of media and entertainment. Option number one: Pull over to the side of the road and feel miserable for the rest of your life. "Bummer, I took a wrong turn and I didn't get to where I wanted to go. I guess

I'm stuck here for good." That's not a good option, but many people are stuck in that rut of thinking.

Option number two: You are too clever to fall for option one and consider the reality that the earth is round! "If I just keep going the wrong direction long enough, I might get to where I intended to go!" You might laugh at that option, but many people live their lives that way. They realize the direction they are going is not right, but they keep on going anyway with the hope that things will turn out alright, regardless of the bad choices.

There's a third option, and that is the one I chose on the night I took a wrong turn in L.A. I found an off ramp, made a U-turn and began heading in the right direction. It's called repentance.

There can be an overwhelming sense of defeat and exasperation when you realize that you have spent time, money and energy going in the wrong direction. Turning around can be a very humbling experience to face.

Sometimes I'll test a group of people and ask them what the main theme of Jesus' preaching was. The common answer is "love", which is definitely a good response, but the Bible says this about the preaching ministry of Jesus, "...from that time Jesus began to preach and say, 'Repent, for the kingdom of heaven is at hand'"[120] "...and that repentance for forgiveness of sins would be proclaimed in His name to all the nations, beginning from Jerusalem."[121] The preaching of repentance did not stop with Jesus but also continued with His disciples, "...but kept declaring both to those of Damascus first, and also at

---

[120] Matthew 3:2
[121] Luke 24:47

Jerusalem and then throughout all the region of Judea, and even to the Gentiles, that they should repent and turn to God, performing deeds appropriate to repentance."[122]

Repentance lies at the foundation of a right relationship with God, and it's more than feeling bad or guilty for what you've done. Repentance means to recognize that you are going in the wrong direction and proceed to turn around and go in the right direction. "For the sorrow that is according to the will of God produces a repentance without regret, leading to salvation, but the sorrow of the world produces death."[123] "Or do you think lightly of the riches of His kindness and tolerance and patience, not knowing that the kindness of God leads you to repentance."[124]

The word repentance has a negative association in some people's minds because of the understanding and importance of repenting of our sins. Unfortunately, they have misunderstood the beauty and wonder of repentance, which is not merely turning away from sin but turning towards God. It is possible that many of you who have taken the time to read this book have been made aware of some media choices and practices in your life that do not follow the footsteps of Jesus. If you have realized that you have been heading down the wrong road and making ignorant or willfully poor decisions, don't hesitate to begin with repentance, "for if we confess our sins, He is faithful and just to forgive us our sins and to cleanse us from all unrighteousness."[125] Many of us have been polluted and need to

---

[122] Acts 26:20

[123] 2 Corinthians 7:10

[124] Romans 2:4

[125] 1 John 1:9

be made clean again with forgiveness offered by God through the sacrifice of His Son Jesus. We need "...repentance without regret, leading to salvation..."[126]

---

[126] 2 Corinthians 7:10

## Scriptures for Chapter 32

"But if we walk in the Light as
He Himself is in the Light, we
have fellowship with one another,
and the blood of Jesus His Son
cleanses us from all sin."

### 1 John 1:7

"I tell you that in the same way,
there will be more joy in heaven over
one sinner who repents than over
ninety-nine righteous persons who
need not repentance." – Jesus

### Luke 15:7

"I have not come to call the righteous
but sinners to repentance." – Jesus

### Luke 5:32

"Therefore bear fruit in
keeping with repentance."

### Matthew 3:8

## Chapter 33: Replace Versus Take Away

The late preacher A.W. Tozer once wrote about the media distractions of his time, circa 1950s, "'Commune with your own heart upon your bed and be still' is a wise and healing counsel, but how can it be followed in this day of the newspaper, the telephone, the radio and the television? These modern playthings, like pet tiger cubs, have grown so large and dangerous that they threaten to devour us all. No spot is now safe from the world's intrusion."

Parents reading this book might come to the revelation that they have allowed things into the home that are now taking over and devouring their family. What do you do? It's not just parents either, maybe you are a young person who realizes that you have been taken captive by media and entertainment. What do you do?

One suggestion is to replace versus take away. Don't merely ax certain things unless you are prepared to replace that activity and time with something better. For parents, this starts with babies and toddlers. It has become way too convenient to put an infant in front of a screen as the electronic baby sitter. According to Dr. Dimitri Christakis, the average age a child begins watching TV in the U.S. is four months old! Why not three months? Because a baby at four months can sit up on their own. That particular issue has been overcome by baby toy manufacturers who have designed bouncy seats and potty chairs to hold a digital tablet. The average child under three years old watches three to five hours of TV each day. When I interviewed

Dr. Dimitri Christakis for my documentary, Captivated, he shared about research, which shows that for every hour a child under three watches TV each day, they are ten percent more likely to develop attention problems by the time they start school. That means that a child watching five hours of TV per day is fifty percent more likely to develop ADD or ADHD compared with the child who doesn't watch any television. What should a parent do instead? If you are a young person what should you do when you are older and start raising a family? Spend that time interacting! Read to them, play with them, sing to them, take lots of strolls, see lots of things; real things. Let them handle real things. This principle of replacing versus taking away works better the younger a child is: setting a better trajectory than letting children orient their lives to a screen. But what if you didn't do that? What if you were oriented to screens as a child and it's your comfort zone?

Unplugging is one step, but filling that new void with something better is the critical follow-up step. The big challenge is that it will take more work. It's convenient to plop on a couch, turn a device on and zone out. It takes more work to plan a craft or an outdoor activity, clear a table to accommodate a puzzle, unearth the board game, put air in the flat tires for a bike ride, plot the journey to the park, assemble the model, fly the kite, read aloud, or endure the process of learning an instrument or listening to someone learn an instrument!

We are not a screen-free family, but my children have grown up without broadcast or cable TV and without video games, and their lives are not boring. They went from playing with toys to making toys in our wood shop. My son and I build and crash model RC airplanes. They all enjoy learning instruments, baking in the kitchen, playing the outdoor game of kubb, and the list could go on. Here's the catch: it means more from Dad and Mom. More time, more energy, and often more money, than passively spending time in front of a screen. The big question is whether or not it is worth the extra effort. I could tell you that it is, but that's not the same as experiencing it for yourself. You'll have to give it a try and begin a new adventure.

What about teens or young adults? This may come close to being something akin to rocket science, which can tend to suffer the agony of launches blowing up. The fear of conflict or failure can paralyze any attempts at making changes in the home.

First, sit down together as a family and talk about this. Share your concerns, your hopes, and your personal mistakes. Share about your own weaknesses and your desire to set a new trajectory in the home. Confess your failure to set certain boundaries earlier in the game, and decide together on a game plan for the future. Bob Waliszewski, director of Plugged In, has a great book on this subject called "Plugged In Parenting." He writes about having a family entertainment constitution.

Have you ever opened a packaged product that was meticulously boxed up in such a way that it is seemingly impossible to get it all back in the box if you decide it's something you would like to return? A similar problem can happen with media choices and certain electronic devices or types of media that have been allowed in the home, only to realize later that it was a door that would have been better left shut. It can be much more challenging to shut a door that should not have been opened in the first place, just like the packaged product that you cannot get back in the box.

The pressure on parents from teens to allow a smartphone or a gaming console may seem to be a continuous battle not worth fighting. The white flag is often raised when parents are overwhelmed by the powerful alliance with new cultural norms: "But everyone has one…" or "But Johnny is allowed…" For many parents who have raised that flag of surrender, they now are faced with a bigger battle of rescuing their POW's caught in the digital conflict. Some war torn families just mourn the defeat and do nothing. Don't surrender. The battle is not against your children. The battle is for their hearts and minds. The war zone has reached our doorsteps and you cannot remain complacent.

In order to win this battle, don't just take things away. Make it a new endeavor to go and enjoy the great outdoors: go throw a Frisbee, swing a bat, catch a ball, take a walk or a hike, ride your bike, smell the flowers, enjoy a sunset, make a snowman, make a pile of leaves and jump in them, fly a kite, build a sand castle, or any other activity you like to do but have not taken the time to enjoy because you are so occupied with your assortment of electronic screens. In the process you'll burn some calories, gain some health and probably feel better about life in general.

## Scriptures for Chapter 33

"Therefore, my beloved brethren, be steadfast, immovable, always abounding in the work of the Lord, knowing that your toil is not in vain in the Lord."

### 1 Corinthians 15:58

"But he who practices the truth comes to the light, so that his deeds may be manifested as having been wrought in God." —Jesus

### John 3:21

"Live the rest of the time in the flesh no longer for the lusts of men, but for the will of God."

### 1 Peter 4:2

"Now flee from youthful lusts and pursue righteousness, faith, love and peace, with those who call upon the Lord from a pure heart."

### 2 Timothy 2:22

## Chapter 34: A Balanced Plate –
## Your Daily Media Diet

I remember a lesson in grade school about a healthy, balanced diet. It was based on our government's daily recommendations, which was illustrated in a diagram known as the USDA food pyramid. The small point at the top was supposed to represent fats, oils, and sweets, which were to be consumed sparingly. The picture of the donut and chocolate chip cookie is what kept my attention. The next level down was divided between milk and meat products. The cheese on the left looked appetizing, but the raw steak on the right side looked gross. Who wants to gnaw on raw meat? Then came the veggies and fruits. The level that I was most comfortable with was the large base representing bread, cereal, rice and pasta—six to eleven servings a day!

The reality was that I didn't have much of a choice. I ate what my mom put on the table or packed in my lunchbox, and that was that. The USDA recently upgraded their balanced diet campaign with new slogans and graphics. It's now known as "My Plate." The presentation is a big improvement, but the recommendations have not changed much. When it comes to the subject of our daily media diet, there has been an exponential change in people's media and entertainment diet with very little progress in wisdom and discernment. There is a need to be concerned about what is on your plate from day to day. This generation is plagued with media gluttony and there's a need for change in the regular daily diet. We need **DIscErnmenT**.

The first step is to scale back on the quantity of media and entertainment that you are consuming as an individual or as a family. How much time do you invest in entertainment? It is not likely that you will steadily become more like Christ if you are captivated with everything else but Him. You tend to become what you behold. "But we all, with unveiled face, beholding as in a mirror the glory of the Lord, are being transformed into the same image from glory to glory, just as from the Lord, the Spirit."[127] Use self-control to limit your media diet and commit to spending more time reading God's word, seeking Him through prayer, and reflecting on the life of Christ. "Therefore be careful how you walk, not as unwise men but as wise, making the most of your time, because the days are evil. So then do not be foolish, but understand what the will of the Lord is."[128]

Be purposeful in your media choices and fill your life with more meaningful activities so you don't have time to just veg out in front of a screen. Nobody will die if you don't watch television every day or several movies every week. It will take discipline to break the habit of defaulting to a screen when you don't have a plan otherwise. Just like going on a food diet, you must be determined and intentional. You'll have to resist the tendency of over consuming until you have established new habits.

Some things in life that are good can become a bad thing if consumed excessively. Our life on earth is remarkably short compared with eternity. Live your life in the light of eternity.

---

[127] 2 Corinthians 3:18
[128] Ephesians 5:15-17

Jesus said, "But I tell you that every careless word that people speak, they shall give an accounting for it in the day of judgment."[129] If careless words are subject to scrutiny, how much more are our actions?

The next step is to focus on quality as well as quantity. If you were on a food diet you would not only be concerned with the amount of food, but the quality of food you were consuming. There is so much "junk food" entertainment being disseminated in the market, and if you consume a steady diet of it you will experience a decline in spiritual health in the long run. Not all movies are garbage; there are some that have Christian themes, good morals, or are helpful, informative, and educational. These choices take wisdom, and that is assuming you can first identify toxic media which is always harmful, and then discern the junk food which should be the smallest portion on the media plate just like the example of the food pyramid.

The following alliteration comes from my seminar. These are all helpful hints to having a balanced media diet in the home.

**Model:** The first piece of advice might be the hardest hill to climb when it comes to providing leadership in your home. Before you can effectively mentor your children in wise media choices and use of technology, you first have to be a living example. Demonstrate that the technology in your life is under your control, instead of you being under its spell. Show that you have a vision and direction for your elective time other than the common default of zoning out in front of a screen. Be willing to set aside your smartphone for intentional periods in order to give your attention to your family. Do not just get home from work and flop down on the couch in front of the TV.

---

[129] Matthew 12:36

**Mentor:** Teach your children (for parents), or your peers (for young adults), or your church (for pastors) the importance of media discernment. Your example will go a long way, but you also need to be intentional about training others in your sphere of influence. Be ready to connect the dots between a relationship with Christ and how that should impact all areas of our lives including media and entertainment.

**Moderate:** Set boundaries in your home (parents) and in your own life. Don't say no to everything but don't say yes to everything either. Choose your battles wisely, but recognize there will be battles worth fighting and ground worth defending.

**Monitor:** You need to keep track of what's happening in your home. This takes a lot of work, but it's one of the jobs a parent is called to do. If you are a young person then you need to monitor your own choices as well and hold them up to the light of Christ for His guidance.

**Move:** Make sure that your trajectory in life is always towards the Lord. Move closer to Him in your heart and in your actions.

**Motivate:** Remember that the goal is to keep your eyes on Christ. Parents need to motivate children out of a passion for Jesus, not just rules of conduct. If you are a young adult and you find that you are experiencing opposition from peers because you don't go along with them in their foolish choices, be sure to diffuse the tension by pointing out that you are motivated by your love for Jesus and your desire to please Him and draw near to Him with a pure conscience. People often think you are judging them if you choose to go a different direction. Let them know your decisions are motivated by love, not judgment. "For the time already past is sufficient for you to have carried out the desire of the Gentiles, having pursued a course of sensuality, lusts, drunkenness, carousing, drinking parties and abominable idolatries. In all this, they are surprised that you do not run with them into the same excesses of dissipation, and they malign you; but they will give account to Him who is ready to judge the living and the dead."[130]

**Mediate:** Spend specific time in prayer about media and entertainment. Ask God for help and wisdom. Be sure to pray for others who are struggling in this area and ask God to open their eyes to their blindness or captivity, so that they will begin seeking Him for true freedom.

**Meditate:** Read the Bible, study the Bible, memorize Bible verses, listen to the Bible being taught and read, and meditate on the Bible. There are so many Biblical principles that apply to the digital age. I have endeavored to include many Bible verses in this book to demonstrate the importance of applying God's word to our lives.

It is really challenging to write a book that is bound to have both a young adult and adult audience. I have endeavored to write as broadly as possible to reach out to teens, young adults, and adults, especially parents. The next chapter is predominately for parents, so if you are not a parent you can skip to the end of the next chapter and there will be a couple of paragraphs just for you. If you want to get a jump on learning important parenting skills while you are still young, then by all means read the whole chapter.

---

[130] 1 Peter 4:3-5

## Scriptures for Chapter 34

"Finally, brethren, whatever is true,
whatever is honorable, whatever is
right, whatever is pure, whatever is
lovely, whatever is of good repute,
if there is any excellence and if
anything worthy of praise,
dwell on these things."

### Philippians 4:8

"For the commandment is a lamp
and the teaching is light; and reproofs
for discipline are the way of life."

### Proverbs 6:23

"But whoever drinks of the water
that I will give him shall never thirst;
but the water that I will give him
will become in him a well of water
springing up to eternal life." – Jesus

### John 4:14

## Chapter 35: Finding Green Pastures in the Digital Age

I used to raise a small number of sheep. It was a ragtag flock with a variety of colors and sizes but they had at least one thing in common: they were often discontent in my inferior pasture and were often escaping to the neighbors' beautiful alfalfa field. I thought I had good fences, but those woolly rascals are smarter and more determined than you might imagine. I couldn't figure out how they were escaping. I walked my fence line and everything seemed sheep proof. Something seemed very fishy about this so I decided to play Sherlock Holmes and conduct a thorough stakeout.

The sheep seemed to have some keen instinct that warned them that they were being watched. They went back to eating the grass on my side of the fence and were acting content. After a long period of watching I was about to give up when the largest ewe looked up from the grass and began gazing around sheepishly. She must have determined that the coast was clear because she proceeded to casually lumber over to a particular spot along the fence. I don't know what I was expecting. I couldn't imagine her pole vaulting over, but they were getting out somehow. For a moment I thought she went back to eating, because her head was down, but suddenly I realized what was happening when she began kicking her back legs furiously in a very comical fashion. She had stuck her head through a low spot under the fence and was trying to push her large body through the small opening with all of her might. I didn't think it was remotely possible until she suddenly popped out the other side, and before I knew it, I was not counting sheep going over a fence, but they were all going under the fence one after another and I was wide awake.

This is the same behavior parents may identify in their children when it comes to regulations in the home. Shepherds throughout the centuries and around the world have cared for large flocks of sheep without any fences. The sheep are protected and provided for by the shepherd's presence. Fences are a poor substitute for Dad's presence and Mom's presence in their children's lives. "These words, which I am commanding you today, shall be on your heart. You shall teach them diligently to your sons and shall talk of them when you sit in your house and when you walk by the way and when you lie down and when you rise up."[131] The following paragraphs are some helpful hints for applying this verse in the home.

### Helpful Hint #1

A simple suggestion I would like to make for parents is to spend more time with your children. Watch appropriate movies or television programs with them and talk about the content and worldview. Sit down with them and have them show you all their video games, and assess them together. Listen to music together and make it a habit to talk about the message in the music. More important than all of these, study the Bible with them and pray with them.

Raising your children for Christ is the most important task that you will ever have in life. Don't drop the ball; you can either let the world's entertainment raise them or you can take

---

[131] Deuteronomy 6:6-7

responsibility for your God-given privilege of leading your children to follow Christ.

## Helpful Hint #2

As you ponder what you are putting on your plate each day, there are some reasonable alternatives to consider. One way to solve the problem of unwanted commercials and family unfriendly programs is to not watch real time TV programming. Instead, make good use of the DVD player or DVR and the growing selection of family friendly films and Christ centered films. New technologies allow you to record your favorite shows and fast forward past the commercials.

## Helpful Hint #3

There is a large variety of Christian music available in nearly every genre. Most of it is available for download or streaming on popular websites, or you can buy CDs at your local Christian bookstore. It may be worth the small subscription fee to have commercial-free streaming.

## Helpful Hint #4

The video games your children play don't have to be violent. If you are determined to let your children waste their time with video games, then do it with non-violent, non-sexual games. Better yet, get a good board game out and play it with them. Take the time to listen to one of my most popular podcast on the Media Talk 101 website called "My Top 5 Concerns about Video Games."[132]

---

[132] www.mediatalk101.org/index.php/Blog/mt101-podcast-ep-006.html

**Helpful Hint #5**

The special boxes or options on video players that allow you to filter bad language are not bad, but they are not the answer to your troubles. They might filter out a sexual word, but it will not filter out the sexual themes in the program, so it is hardly a silver bullet. Most of these new devices do not filter out the bad worldview. If they did filter out bad worldview then you would likely be staring at a blank screen for most of the time. In fact, I'm only familiar with one device that can do such a thing consistently and accurately. It is called the off button and most electronics come equipped with one.

**Helpful Hint #6**

Make a commitment to be devoted to personal prayer for your own needs and also for others and their struggles. Consider organizing a weekly or monthly prayer group to join with you. Study what the Bible says about prayer; it will probably take a long time because there is a lot of material. I compiled a list of Scriptures on prayer and wrote them all down in a notebook that I pick up and read occasionally. I will rarely get through all the verses without stopping to pray because God's Word is so inspiring.

**Helpful Hint #7**

The best time to make decisions about what road to choose is not when you're under pressure to make a choice, but long before you face that guaranteed pressure. Do some research ahead of time. One example of this would be to commit to reading a Christian critique of a movie before inadvertently exposing yourself to compromising media. One of my favorite websites is Pluggedin.com for reading reviews of movies, videos, television programs, and music, from a Christian perspective.

## Helpful Hint #8

If you are struggling with internet porn, you need to install some accountability software or filtering software on your computer. You may even need to cancel your internet subscription. Get an accountability partner and seek godly counsel if you find that you are trapped.

## Helpful Hint #9

You may want to consider cancelling your cable or satellite TV subscription. You might even want to shock everyone and get rid of your TV. Is that legal? Yes!

## Helpful Hint #10

If there is an area of your life that is out of control, you need to get some help. Meet with a responsible adult, a Pastor, or someone recommended by your Pastor for accountability, mentoring and prayer support. "Obey your leaders and submit to them, for they keep watch over your souls as those who will give an account. Let them do this with joy and not with grief, for this would be unprofitable for you."[133]

## Helpful Hint #11

It is important for spiritual growth to be part of a spiritually healthy Christian community.

---

[133] Hebrews 13:17

"And let us consider how to stimulate one another to love and good deeds, not forsaking our own assembling together, as is the habit of some, but encouraging one another; and all the more as you see the day drawing near."[134]

"So we, who are many, are one body in Christ, and individually members one of another."[135]

## Helpful Hint #12

It has been stated several times already, but you can't hear it too much: study God's word. You will not be able to follow Christ if you don't know who He is and what He taught for us to follow.

"You, however, continue in the things you have learned and become convinced of, knowing from whom you have learned them, and that from childhood you have known the sacred writings which are able to give you the wisdom that leads to salvation through faith which is in Christ Jesus. All Scripture is inspired by God and profitable for teaching, for reproof, for correction, for training in righteousness; so that the man of God may be adequate, equipped for every good work."[136]

## Helpful Hints for Teens #1

Some homes do not have any rules about media and some do. If you are still living with your parents, you need to honor

---

[134] Hebrews 10:24-25

[135] Romans 12:5

[136] 2 Timothy 3:14-17

their rules. If they have no rules then you need to adopt some for yourself and demonstrate the life of Christ with sincerity and humility.

"I said to the children in the wilderness, 'Do not walk in the statutes of your fathers or keep their ordinances or defile yourselves with their idols. I am the Lord your God; walk in My statutes and keep My ordinances and observe them.'"[137]

"Let no one look down on your youthfulness, but rather in speech, conduct, love, faith and purity, show yourself an example of those who believe."[138]

**Helpful Hints for Teens #2**

Another great place to start is to think about what it means to follow Jesus. Walking in His footsteps, and looking to Him as the ultimate role model. Have you ever thought about what the Bible teaches about Jesus when He was a child?

"And the Child grew and became strong in spirit, filled with wisdom; and the grace of God was upon Him."[139] Notice that Jesus was filled with wisdom. If that was important for Jesus then it should be important for you as well. What do we know about Jesus as a teen? You are probably thinking... "Does the Bible teach us about Jesus as a teen?" Yes! In fact, we know at least six things about Jesus when He was between the age of twelve and thirty years old.

---

[137] Ezekiel 20:18-19

[138] 1 Timothy 4:12

[139] Luke 2:40

"Then he went down with them and returned to Nazareth; and he remained in submission to them. His mother continued to treasure all these things in her heart."[140] The first thing we learn is that Jesus was in submission to His parents. If anyone could get a pass on submitting to parents, I think it would be the Son of God, but we find just the opposite. He didn't get a pass, He passed along an enduring testimony to other young people of humble submission.

The second thing we learn is from Mark 6:3 which says, "Is this not the carpenter, the Son of Mary, and brother of James, Joses, Judas, and Simon? And are not His sisters here with us?" At the age of twelve, it was normative for a boy to focus on learning the trade of his father. You should be developing useful skills that will help you be a productive adult.

The last four things we learn about Jesus during this time period of His life comes from the following verse: "And Jesus kept increasing in wisdom and stature, and in favor with God and men."[141] The subject of wisdom comes up again. You must pursue wisdom. If Jesus increased in wisdom then you should follow in His example. This verse also tells us that Jesus increased in stature. That is not merely about growing taller, but about becoming more manly or womanly and responsible. It is about increasing in maturity as you get older. There is so much immaturity in our culture today and many adults have not put away childish things. Don't embrace the low expectations for young people in this culture—grow up! Reject mediocrity and laziness. Embrace hard work, responsibility and maturity.

---

[140] Luke 2:51

[141] Luke 2:52

We are also told that Jesus grew in favor with God and men. There are many Scriptures about favor with God. Be sure to study those verses and apply them to your life. When it comes to growing in favor with men, that does not mean that Jesus was seeking peer approval. It means that Jesus was respected and admired by others. He was the kind of person that others liked to be around. They recognized His wisdom, His maturity, and His favor with God.

These six truths about Jesus during His youth provide a great example for you to follow. Aspire to be like Jesus in all of these areas and let them be a filter for all of your media and entertainment choices. Ask yourself the questions, will this help me grow in wisdom? Will my choices help me become more mature? Does this help me grow in favor with God? Do my media choices reflect all of these areas to the people around me? Am I submitting to my parents and other authorities in my life? Does the entertainment I watch help me to be better prepared to be a productive person in society and the home?

## Scriptures for Chapter 35

"Hear, O Israel: The LORD our God, the LORD is one! You shall love the LORD your God with all your heart, with all your soul, and with all your strength.

"And these words which I command you today shall be in your heart. You shall teach them diligently to your children, and shall talk of them when you sit in your house, when you walk by the way, when you lie down, and when you rise up."

### Deuteronomy 6:4-7 NKJV

"Let love be without hypocrisy. Abhor what is evil. Cling to what is good."

### Romans 12:9

## Chapter 36: Finding Freedom

One of the most notable escape stories during World War II took place at the German POW camp, Stalag Luft III and was memorialized in the 1963 film "The Great Escape." Of the seventy-six who escaped through the elaborate tunnel, seventy-three were recaptured and fifty of them were executed on Hitler's orders.

Yet, many are unaware of a previous escape story, which was equally heroic, considerably more outlandish, essentially more effective, and from the very same German camp. Flight Lieutenants Eric Williams, Michael Codner, and Oliver Philpot plotted an escape that Lieutenant Philpot initially discounted as "crackers."

With the help of other POW's, the men constructed a makeshift wooden gymnastics horse, which they carried to a spot each day near a perimeter fence. The prisoners used this for exercise but it also proved to be entertaining to the prison guards. Unbeknownst to the guards, one of the men had been concealed inside this horse and had begun digging. The entrance to the tunnel was covered each day, and the prisoner would be carried back inside the horse. Another man would be carried back to the same spot the next day. Eventually they carried two men at a time to work in tandem. It took over one hundred days to construct one hundred feet of tunnel but in the end, the three made a successful escape to freedom.

I love a good escape story when it's the good guys who find freedom. What compelled these men to endure such extremes and take such risks? I believe their desire for freedom exceeded their fear of death. Their longing for liberty proved stronger than the barbed wire fences, and their dogged determination greater than the guards who sought to hold them captive.

How about you? Have you found yourself captive and longing for freedom? You might be thinking, "Captive? What do you mean by that? I'm not a captive!" That's the response Jesus got when He began teaching others about gaining freedom.

"Then Jesus said to those Jews who believed Him, 'If you abide in My word, you are My disciples indeed. And you shall know the truth, and the truth shall make you free.' They answered Him, 'We are Abraham's descendants, and have never been in bondage to anyone. How can You say, 'You will be made free'?"[142]

Their perspective of freedom was skewed to say the least. The Roman Empire held occupation of Palestine when Jesus spoke those words, not to mention their history of captivity to the Assyrians, the Babylonians, the Medes and Persians, Alexander the Great, and their most notable captivity in Egypt. Yet, that was not the kind of captivity Jesus was trying to teach them about. They missed the spiritual perspective that Christ came to reveal.

Is it possible that His words might apply to you and your situation? Could it be that you are blind to your captivity, or complacent about it, or worse yet, comfortable in it? Many people are escaping today, but not from bondage to freedom; they are escaping from reality to a life of virtual captivity. They

---

[142] John 8:31-33

have been taken hostage through the subtle lure of today's amusements and diversions.

This kind of captivation is often cloaked in deception, which leaves the victim paralyzed without awareness of the true circumstance. It is like the sting of a spider that numbs its prey, yet keeps it alive until all the life is sucked out of it.

Real freedom comes to those who see the chains they are in and find the way of escape. I believe that many are awakening to the reality that they are living in a cage, even though they can't exactly define what it is. Like a captive bird longing to fly, deep down inside they sense that there is something they are missing.

"But God be thanked that though you were slaves of sin, yet you obeyed from the heart that form of doctrine to which you were delivered. And having been set free from sin, you became slaves of righteousness... But now having been set free from sin, and having become slaves of God, you have your fruit to holiness, and the end, everlasting life."[143]

True freedom does not mean doing whatever you please or whatever gratifies you personally. That is the deceptive philosophy of the world that has taken the masses captive. Authentic freedom is about being set free from sin, through Christ, in order to live a holy life that glorifies God. Freedom is escaping sin's penalty, its power, and ultimately its presence to be a child of God and servant of righteousness. This is where life to its fullest begins!

How do you break free and stay free?

---

[143] Romans 6:17-18, 22

"No temptation has overtaken you except such as is common to man; but God is faithful, who will not allow you to be tempted beyond what you are able, but with the temptation will also make the *WAY OF ESCAPE*, that you may be able to bear it. Therefore, my beloved, *FLEE FROM IDOLATRY.*"[144]

One "way of escape" is to flee from idolatry. Now, if you only think of idolatry as people showing reverence by bowing down and making sacrifices to statues of false deities, then you have a narrow view of idolatry. "Therefore consider the members of your earthly body as dead to immorality, impurity, passion, evil desire, and greed, which amounts to idolatry."[145]

Have you allowed today's entertainment and the constant distraction of media to become an idol in your life? If you don't know, here's a simple test that might help—are you willing and ready to let go of it? If thinking about that makes you cringe and react defensively by crafting arguments in your mind to justify how unnecessary it is for you to let anything go, then it might be an indication of idolatry. This is what really hit home with me over twenty-five years ago as a young believer still in my teens when my heart was challenged with the issue of media. I had heard a powerful and convicting sermon about living for Jesus, and the Holy Spirit began to confront me about entertainment.

Do you want real freedom? Are you desperate enough to take some risk and make a move? Are you ready to get past the prison fences and run for your life and gain a new identity? Are

---

[144] 1 Corinthians 10:13-14 (emphasis mine)

[145] Colossians 3:5

you wondering where to start? Well, it's not as difficult as tunneling under prison fences while under the watch of Nazi guards. You can start where I began and take a disciplined break from the unnecessary distractions for a season.

Use the time you'll gain to seek the heart of God about entertainment and media use in your life. Ask Him for wisdom and help to discern how to live your life unfettered by unnecessary and unhealthy choices and habits.

This is not for the faint of heart, but for those whose desire for Christ has become greater than the blockades and distractions of this world. Run for freedom and don't look back. Let your motivation come from a focus on Jesus and let your passion and practice be consumed with pursuing Him and following in His steps.

"Let us lay aside every weight, and the sin which so easily ensnares us, and let us run with endurance the race that is set before us, looking unto Jesus, the author and finisher of our faith..."[146]

Are you free to give your attention to the relationships that God has given you stewardship of, or is your attention held hostage by media? Are you free to redeem the time, or are you a captive to wasting time? Are you free to worship God, or are you captive to idolatry? Do you have a clean conscience or has the temple been defiled? Are you free to think Biblically, or have you been taken captive by philosophies and empty deceptions in

---

[146] Hebrews 12:1-2

the world? Are you free to see God more clearly, or is your heart and mind cluttered with distractions?

My attempt at addressing the issue of media discernment has not been with the goal of being exhaustive but hopefully inspiring. It would be impossible to cover all the different angles and discussions surrounding the subject of media in one book. You have all of the necessary resources available to you in order to honor God in your life. You have the example of Jesus, the truth of the Scriptures, the guidance and power of the Holy Spirit, the testimony of others who are living it and eternal motivation to inspire your direction and fruitfulness for God's Kingdom. As the saying goes, "You can lead a horse to water but you can't make him drink." I have attempted to point you in the right direction but only you can decide whether you will walk the path.

Lastly, surrender your life to Christ and follow him. This is what I have been attempting to communicate in this book all along. What God has planned for you is all that will ever satisfy. It's not just about a willingness to surrender spiritually harmful media habits, it's about letting go in order to abide in Christ.

## Scriptures for Chapter 36

"For whoever will call on the name of the Lord will be saved."

### Romans 10:13

"For by grace you have been saved through faith; and that not of yourselves, it is the gift of God."

### Ephesians 2:8

"If you confess with your mouth the Lord Jesus and believe in your heart that God has raised Him from the dead, you will be saved. For with the heart one believes unto righteousness, and with the mouth confession is made unto salvation."

### Romans 10:9-10

Visit **www.mediatalk101.org** to listen to more than 50 podcasts on the subject of media discernment in the light of following Christ.

Don't miss one of Phillip Telfer's most popular podcasts: Episode #6 "My Top Five Concerns about Video Games"

R00141

Made in the USA
Lexington, KY
19 November 2017